Fish catch at Hague's Resort. Ray Hague Collection,
Museum & Arts Center in the Sequim-Dungeness Valley.

Dedicated to the past,
present and future people
of the Sequim-Dungeness Valley
and celebrating their stories
and the culinary bounty of the region.

Blackberries, Dandelions & Dungeness Crab

WE ARE VERY EXCITED to be able to offer this cookbook as part of our Centennial Celebration! There have been many events throughout the Centennial year that provided opportunities for community-wide participation. This cookbook is a geat example of the Sequim-Dungeness Valley Community Spirit. We would like to thank everyone who submitted a recipe and shared a little information about their personal lives with their stories. We hope you enjoy this book as much as we enjoyed putting it together.

Bon Appétit!

Karen Kuznek-Reese
Centennial Committee Chair
City Clerk

CITY OF
SEQUIM

The People and Food
of the Sequim-Dungeness Valley

Blackberries, Dandelions & Dungeness Crab

The Cookbook of the Century

Celebrating
The City of Sequim's
First 100 Years

SPONSORED BY THE CITY OF SEQUIM

SMALL, FRIENDLY RURAL TOWNS and good food are synonymous. Sequim, to me, has always been about social gatherings. Whether meeting for coffee in the morning before work, drinks at the end of a busy day, or friends engaging each other around the dinner table, it seems like cooking, family and friends are always at the center of life.

This isn't surprising as the Sequim-Dungeness Valley is rich in opportunity to gather and harvest the ingredients of a great meal. In fact the name the first settlers, the Jamestown S'Klallam people, gave to this place "Sequim" means just that: abundant hunting grounds. It seems life here has always been about food.

Here you can hunt for game in the surrounding wilderness, gather shellfish in the local bays and tidelands, pick succulent wild berries everywhere, and of course cultivate just about anything in the temperate arid valley with the genius of irrigation. It is no wonder that all of us who choose to call this remarkable place home are frequently gathered around the table enjoying great food. Today this local bounty gives us great gourmet food in a variety of eateries but it is still the comfort food of family meals that resonates most with me.

Interestingly this cookbook isn't so much about those great old (and new) comfort food recipes as much as it is about the stories behind them and the memories they recall; stories of the wonderful, connected small town experience shared by all who live here, whether for generations or newly arrived.

I hope you will be embraced by the spirit embodied in this charming little book; try a few recipes, let the stories wash over you like a soothing late summer breeze, and be transported, at least for a moment, to a kinder, gentler time.

Ken Hays, Mayor
City of Sequim

Blackberries, Dandelions & Dungeness Crab

The Cookbook of the Century

Produced for
The City of Sequim
by
Joseph Robert Cowles
and
Barbora Holan Cowles

Production Management:
Barbara Collier Hanna

Cover Photograph:
Cays Family Reunion pictured on postcard
dated October 19, 1912. Susan Goff Collection,
Courtesy of the Museum & Arts Center
in the Sequim-Dungeness Valley

Image of apple basket on page 116
was adapted from a woodblock print by
Dutch illustrator Anton Pietck (1895-1987)

In an effort to respect the voices of the authors, the stories and recipes in this book have been printed as submitted unless an obvious error was detected. Minor typos and punctuation were corrected. If a major error or missing component was found, every effort was made to contact the author for clarification.

Fish catch at old hatchery with the Dawleys and Cooks, circa 1918.
Mary Dittmer Collection,
Museum & Arts Center in the Sequim-Dungeness Valley.

Contents

Photograph courtesy of the Museum & Arts Center in the Sequim-Dungeness Valley

Appetizers and Beverages

Bailey's Cream

Submitted by Renee Lemmon Bleile

4 eggs
1/2 teaspoon vanilla extract
2 drops coconut extract
2 Tablespoons chocolate syrup
1 bottle Avoset Cream (do NOT use whipping cream!)
1 can Eagle Brand Milk
1-1/3 cup whiskey
Blend together for 3 minutes

PENINSULA LOOKBACK
from the *Peninsula Daily News, 1958*

50 YEARS AGO: Miles Lemmon celebrated his
90th birthday yesterday as Clallam Lodge No. 72,
International Order of Odd Fellows, honored him with
a party in the IOOF hall on First Street in Port Angeles.
Lemmon was born in Vermillion County, Indiana,
in 1868, and his family moved to Sequim via Missouri
in 1890. He married Marissa Cays of the old Dungeness
pioneer family in November 1895.

Lemmon was a carpenter for several years, then became
a farmer and worked for the city of Port Angeles for
16-1/2 years before retiring at age 75.

Marissa Cays Lemmon Roberson and Miles D. Lemmon.

Barb's Famous Cheese Ball

Submitted by Barbara Collier Hanna

2 packages (8 oz. each) cream cheese
1 can crushed pineapple in its own juice
1/4 cup green pepper, finely chopped
2 Tbsp. white onion, finely chopped
1 Tbsp. seasoning salt
1 to 1-1/2 cups chopped walnuts

Bring cream cheese to room temperature to soften. Drain the pineapple well. Save the juice for another purpose. Mix together all ingredients well, except the walnuts. You can use a spoon, but hands work much better for the job. Form the mixture into a ball, place in a bowl and cover tightly over the ball with plastic wrap. Refrigerate overnight. Right before serving, roll the ball in the chopped walnuts. Serve with crackers and vegetables. Triscuits and baby carrots are my favorites.

A rare photo: cooking with friends Katy and Barb in the 1980's.

WHEN I WAS IN COLLEGE at Washington State University, I spent the first half of my senior year living in Seattle and doing an internship with Nordstrom in their corporate sales promotion office. One of my jobs was to help organize the big fall fashion promotion. After the week-long event was over, things slowed down a bit and one day a co-worker brought in some recipes to sort through. I can't imagine this happening now, but at the time, no one seemed to be bothered by it. I wasn't very interested in food and cooking at the time, but a couple of her recipes seemed interesting and I thought I'd try them. I think I first made this cheese ball for a holiday party with friends. It was a huge hit and really easy, so I took it to parties, picnics, and showers for years. After a while, I became famous for it. I still make it for family gatherings. It is one of my mother-in-law's favorite dishes and she always requests it for the holidays and her birthday.

Clam and Crab Roll-ups

Submitted by Patti J. Mower

As printed in a "Kitchen Korner" article
by Marian Platt in the *Sequim Gazette*

*Patti took Second Place honors in the
1994 Pacific Northwest Clam Chowder Cook-off
with her Clam and Crab Roll-ups*

Preheat oven to 350F. Roll 2 sheets phyllo dough thin.
Mix 1 can chopped clams and 1/3 cup flaked crabmeat,
1/2 cup chopped celery, 1/3 cup mayonnaise, 4 oz.
cream cheese, 1/2 cup shredded mozzarella cheese,
1 heaping teaspoon minced onion, 1/4 cup combined
basil and finely chopped green and red peppers,
1/2 clove garlic, minced, and 1/4 cup Parmesan cheese
in large bowl; thoroughly combine ingredients, mixing
with hands if necessary. Spread on Phyllo dough,
avoiding edges. Roll up and place on ungreased baking
sheet. Bake at 350F until golden brown, about 20-30
minutes; cheese mixture may bubble out of ends.
Allow to slightly cool, then slice and serve with
fresh lemon slices. A unique appetizer or main dish.

Crab and Artichoke Dip

Submitted by Patti J. Mower

1 package (8 oz.) cream cheese
1 can quartered artichoke pieces
1/2 cup mayonnaise
1/2 cup fresh sliced green onions
1/2 to 1 tsp. seasoning salt
1/2 tsp. red pepper flakes or 1 heaping tsp.
    Mrs. Dash's spicy seasoning
1/2 to 2/3 cup shredded cheddar
    —sharp or medium, not mild
1/2 cup shredded mozzarella
1/2 cup grated parmesan
1 to 2 large crabs, shucked
    —try to keep the pieces large and whole
1/4 cup dry white wine (optional)

Combine all ingredients except the crab in a medium
to large bowl, squish with your hands until smooth and
well blended. Gently fold in the crab so as not to break
down the pieces. Sprinkle top with a little more grated
cheddar and put in the oven at 350 degrees for 15 to 20
minutes. Finish by broiling until starting to brown.
Remove and serve with chewy French rolls, crackers
or whatever.

To make a great Oscar, you may omit the artichokes
and put in spinach or asparagus to top grilled halibut.

Dungeness Bay for the best crab.

Creamy Crab and Artichoke Spread

Submitted by Patsy Mattingley

1 cup cooked crab meat
1 8-ounce package cream cheese
      (at room temperature)
1 cup mayonnaise
1/3 cup chopped onions
1 can (13.75 ounce) artichoke hearts,
      (drained and chopped)
3/4 cup shredded Parmesan cheese
French bread or crackers for spreading

Preheat oven to 375 degrees. In medium mixing bowl,
blend together cream cheese and mayonnaise
until smooth. Stir in remaining ingredients
and place mixture in glass pie plate.

Bake, uncovered, for 15 to 18 minutes,
until heated through and lightly browned.

Serve with crackers or French Bread.

"The longer you keep it, the better it tastes."

Mom's Raspberry "Jump"

Submitted by Bob Stipe

6 cups fresh raspberries
6 cups white sugar
6 cups cheap vodka

Mash berries
(room temperature),
stir in sugar and let sit
(with occasional stir) until sugar is dissolved.
Add vodka and stir together for a few minutes.
Pour into bottle with tight lid or cork and refrigerate
for a minimum of 6 months. (Turn bottle upside down
and shake gently every week to blend ingredients.)

When ready for use, pour the needed amount through
a fine strainer to catch the seeds, then serve chilled
in a liqueur glass or over ice cream (my favorite).
Mom used to keep this for years under the sink in
her kitchen but Judy and I like it kept in the refrigerator
because it keeps its red color. The longer you keep it, the
better it tastes.

Dedicated with love to Mom from her son Bob Stipe.

MARY LORETTA MILLER'S FAMILY moved to Sequim in 1926 and bought a farm south of Carlsborg. She attended Carlsborg School in 1927 and Sequim Schools from 1929-1937. Mary also helped her parents on their farm until she married William Lloyd Stipe in 1937. They worked farms on Lost Mountain & Riverside Road (River Road today), until her marriage to Ted Schott—when they began "Schott's Produce" on the Cays Road.

Mary was famous for her peas and shipped them to Victoria, Seattle and local markets. She ran the entire operation with the help of her children while Ted traveled with construction jobs. She later grew and sold blueberries commercially. My mother was an amazing cook and made most of the meals from her garden, in addition to being a Life Member of Sequim Garden Club and Sequim Prairie Grange. The Irrigation Festival chose her as one of their Honorary Pioneers in 2009.

Dandelion Wine

Submitted by Richard and Karen Grimsley

Clean and thoroughly wash 5 gallon crock.
Place in crock:

> 2 quarts dandelion blossoms
> > (picked with no green stems)
> 1 gallon boiling water

Let mixture stand 24 hours and then strain
through a clean cheesecloth.

Then add:

> 3-1/2 lbs. sugar
> 2 lemons
> 2 oranges
> 1 cup raisins
> 1 yeast cake

Mix thoroughly, cover loosely and let stand
until fermentation stops; then strain.
Let stand for a day. Then bottle but don't seal tightly.
Keep mixture warm during fermentation process.

THIS RECIPE FOR Dandelion Wine has been
in the Grimsley family for generations, beginning
with Great Grandmother Hellman, who lived in
Michigan. My husband's family dairy farmed
in Agnew and both his mother and grandmother
continued to make this wine over the years.

Their dairy farm had an abundance of lush
dandelion blossoms. His parents and grandparents
are long since gone, but we continued to make
the wine occasionally when we could talk our kids
into harvesting the dandelion blossoms around
our home in Port Angeles. The wine has a fruity taste
and is quite sweet. It is imperative to pick the blossoms
carefully because any green vegetation adds bitterness.

Reportedly the first creamery truck in the Dungeness Valley.
Virginia Keeting Collection,
Museum & Arts Center in the Sequim-Dungeness Valley.

Condiments

Glenna's Favorite Zucchini Relish

Submitted by Linda Livingston

10 cups chopped zucchini
    (good use of overgrown zucchini)
4 cups onion, chopped
1 each red and green bell peppers, chopped
2-1/2 cups apple cider vinegar
4 cups sugar
1/2 teaspoon pepper
1 teaspoon each mustard seed, celery seed,
    turmeric and nutmeg
3 tablespoons salt
2 tablespoons cornstarch

In a large glass or heavy plastic container combine zucchini, onions and peppers with 3 tablespoons of salt and let set overnight. In the morning, rinse well and drain thoroughly. Add vinegar, sugar, pepper, mustard seed, celery seed, turmeric and nutmeg.

In an 8-quart pot bring the mixture to a bubbling boil, turn it down to simmer and let it simmer 20 minutes.

Mix 2 tablespoons cornstarch with 1/2 cup water, stir in well to thicken. Pour into pint or half-pint jars and seal in a hot water bath for 10 minutes. Makes 6 pints or 12 half-pints.

Glenna taught me how to cook and can everything in sight.

GLENNA NEWLUN LIVINGSTON came to the Sequim valley in the early 1940's as a young bride and lived on a dairy farm in Sequim the rest of her life. Glenna was an inspiration to her family in and out of the kitchen. She was a lady who was open and caring with everyone she met and always looked for the best in others.

She was an excellent cook and many ate at her table through the years. There was always room to set another plate. When I married her son, Larry, my kitchen expertise was that I could open a mean can of soup and cook hot dogs. Glenna taught me how to cook and can everything in sight. Her daughters also learned how to cook and can with Glenna while growing up, and they continue those family traditions.

At the time she taught us to make this relish we chopped it all by hand, and it took hours to get it as small as it needed to be. We usually made a double batch, often a triple batch. In later years, a blender or food processor made the chopping so much easier.

Ruthella and Louise Potter.

Lemon Sauce

Submitted by Louise Potter

Mix well in sauce pan:
1 cup sugar
2 tablespoons corn starch
Add 2 cups boiling water and boil 1 minute
        ... then add
4 tablespoons butter
2 teaspoons lemon juice (fresh or bottled)
1 tablespoon lemon peel
Keep sauce warm and serve over brown
bread, date roll, or stale cake

*"Sequim is a place where people
take time to talk with others
and where people are just
downright neighborly."*

I CAME TO SEQUIM from Michigan in 2007, and
was thrilled when my then 93-year old mother agreed
to move here with me. We felt like two adventurers.

As we settled in our new homes, we discovered that
we had journeyed to a town just like the neighborhood
I grew up in during the 50's. Sequim is a place where
people take time to talk with others and where people
are just downright neighborly. With the mountains
and blue sky, we both felt like we had moved inside
a postcard.

At our first Lavender Festival, Mom wanted to share
the family quilt from the 1880's. This family quilt was
passed from my mother's grandmother through four
generations to me. Like my mother and her mother,
I have this quilt hanging on my bedroom wall.

Mom shared quilts and recipes with her two daughters.
One family favorite is this recipe for lemon sauce,
which, like the quilt, came from her grandmother.
Mom used the sauce on brown bread and on
"more mature" cake.

No Fail Blender Hollandaise

Submitted by Berta Warden

Dungeness Barnhouse Bed and Breakfast

4 large egg yolks
4 teaspoons lemon juice
2/3 cup butter, melted to bubbling
2 teaspoons hot water (if needed to thin)

Place egg yolks and lemon juice in small blender container. Cover and process at medium speed until blended.

With motor running, add butter in a thin stream. The mixture will thicken as butter is added. A little hot water may be added if needed to thin sauce to pouring consistency.

Serve immediately.

"Great with Dungeness Crab and Portabello Mushroom Benedict"—see page 62.

Walt's Tartar Sauce

Submitted by Celeste Kardonsky Dybeck

1 cup mayonnaise
1 Tbsp. yellow mustard
1 large grated dill pickle
About 1-2 Tbsp. pickle juice
1/2 cup grated onion with the juice
1 hardboiled egg, grated
Squeeze of fresh lemon juice if you have it on hand

Toss the mayo into a medium bowl.
Add the rest of the ingredients.

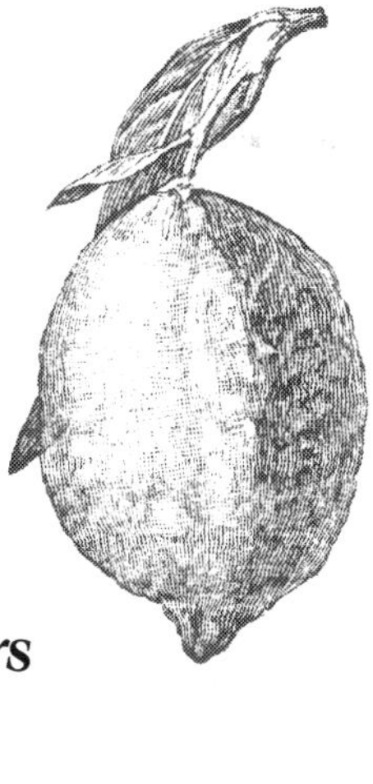

Dad always said, "Make it early so it can set for a few hours before dinner. It will taste a lot better."

Strawberry Rhubarb Jam

Submitted by Priscilla Hudson

2-1/2 cups fresh or frozen strawberries, crushed
1-1/2 cups finely diced fresh or frozen rhubarb
2-1/2 cups sugar
1 cup (8 ounces) crushed pineapple, undrained
1 package (3 ounces) strawberry gelatin

In a large kettle, combine strawberries, rhubarb, sugar, and pineapple. Bring to a boil; reduce heat and simmer for 20 minutes. Remove from heat; stir in gelatin until dissolved. Pour into refrigerator containers, leaving half inch headspace. Let stand until cooled to room temperature. Top with lids. Can refrigerate 3-4 weeks. Yields 5 1/2 cups.

I GREW UP IN Michigan and this was my mom's recipe. I recall she always had some available when I returned for a visit from nursing school.

I moved to the Northwest in 1964 and retired in Sequim in 2004.

Uncooked Apple Sauce

Submitted by Melvina Worman

With so many apples in our area, I wanted to submit an unusual Apple Sauce recipe. A few years ago, I told a healthy eating chef I needed to cook apple sauce. He surprised me by saying, "Why cook it?" I have had it raw ever since. It will last in the fridge for around 10 to 12 days.

Washed apples, cored and cut up to fill vita-mix
1/2 cup water
1 tsp. Cinnamon, or more to taste
1/4 agave, or more to taste
1 tsp. vanilla if you like

Add the water first, then the cored, cut apples, cinnamon, agave, and vanilla. Blend on low, increase speed to high, for about 30-40 seconds, using plunger to push down. A blender also may be used, making less at a time.

That's all there is to a tasty nutritional dish, easy, and always welcome at a potluck!

Enjoy!

Wayne's Sauce
For Salmon Barbecuing

Submitted by Patsy Mattingley

1/4 pound butter, melted
4 tablespoons soy sauce
1 teaspoon Worcestershire sauce
2 or 3 cloves crushed garlic
2 tablespoons catsup
1 tablespoon yellow mustard
Mix all ingredients.

Dredge salmon fillets in mixture. Grill salmon.

Dave Jensen preparing the salmon for Wayne's Sauce.

Barbecuing the salmon.

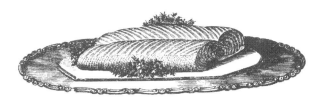

Annie Nerbovig with cows. Ginger Alexander Collection,
Museum & Arts Center in the Sequim-Dungeness Valley.

Soups and Stews

Beef Minestrone Soup

Submitted by Patti J. Mower

1 to 1-1/2 lbs. ground beef
1 handful sliced pepperoni
1 handful sliced salami
1/4 cup chopped white onion
2 to 3 garlic cloves chopped
1 jar (e.g. *Classico*) marinara or spicy spaghetti sauce
1 can garbanzo beans
1 can cut green beans
1 can red kidney beans
1 can beef consommé
2 to 3 red small/medium potatoes cubed
1 cup spiral, penne, or macaroni
      slightly cooked to al dente
1 carrot, sliced
1 zucchini, sliced
1 small handful of Italian seasoning (unsalted)
1 handful of Italian cheeses, grated

Brown the ground beef along with the salami and pepperoni and drain. Place in a crock pot and pour the jar of marina sauce over the meat, along with the consommé. Mix together and add the rest of the above items and leave for 1 to 2 hours, watch for bubbling, then turn down to low heat. Don't be afraid to add 1/2 glass of red wine if you want.

"Please try it by this recipe before changing ingredients and the way you make it. Just leave out the things you hate."

Close to Pelican Pub & Brewery Chili

Submitted by Patti J. Mower

This will fill a large pot. Read the whole recipe before starting.

Buy a tiny brown bag of the greatest chili spices ever formulated—"Carroll Shelby's Chili Kit." Ask for it if you can't find it. It's the foundation of the whole thing and can't be beat.

Cut up 1 to 1-1/2 lbs. of sirloin or other steak into pieces about the size of M&M's. Brown 1/3 of the bits of meat at a time in olive oil, sprinkled with part of the chili powder Carroll provided and put it in the pot.

Chop "fine" (no big chunks):

> 1/2 medium sized onion (red, sweet, or regular)
> 1 small pasilla pepper
> A couple of garlic cloves
> A big ripe fresh tomato

Put these goodies in the beef browning pan with some more olive oil and sprinkle more of Carroll's powder on them. Cook at medium heat until opaque. Put it in the pot with the meat (don't get the idea you can cook the meat and the goodies together.) Put the pot on medium-low heat.

Time to open cans and dump the ingredients into the pot:

> 1 – 14 oz. can diced tomatoes
> 1 – 7 3/4 oz. can *La Pato* Tomato Sauce
>   (it has a kick to it)
> 2 cans Campbell's Beef Consommé
> 2 cans dark red kidney beans
> 2 cans Chipotle flavored chili beans
>
> The rest of Carroll's chili powder and the salt and cayenne in the packet. Throw out thickener.

Time for the dried peppers—don't panic like I did, Rick Bayless (a great Mexican cuisine chef) bailed us out. It's like duck soup, first you get the duck. Take a couple peppers out of the bag, break off the stem end and shake out the seeds. Put the pods in a dry frying pan on medium low heat and your nose will tell you when to flip them. After they become aromatic on both sides, cover them in water in the frying pan, turn off the heat and let them sit for a while. *Drain away the delicious-looking bitter hateful red water!*

Now you need to get the pods into a paste. (I use a small food processor with some olive oil poured in. A mortar and pestle would work, or just smash them however you can.) Add them to the pot. They add flavor like no other. I know this sounds like a big deal, but it really makes the chili what it is.

Jose's Famous Salsa Chili

Submitted by Mark Ozias and Lisa Boulware

This is the chili we serve regularly at The Red Rooster Grocery. Using *Jose's Famous Salsa* as your base makes this recipe extra easy (no prep work!) and extra delicious. We've found that a "Gringo Mild" chili can be eaten by just about anybody, while a "Hot" or "Crazy Hot" chili can send flames out the ears of sensitive types. This chili is best served with cornbread. If you prefer meat in your chili, simply replace the TSP with 1 lb of browned ground beef (grass-fed of course!)

3 large (quart) containers Jose's Famous Salsa
1 15 oz. can kidney beans
1 15 oz. can black beans
1 15 oz. can pinto beans
1 Tbsp.. olive oil
1 Tbsp.. + 1 tsp. chili powder
2 tsp. cumin
1/4 tsp. allspice
3 cloves garlic, minced
3 cups vegetable or chicken broth
1/2 cup TSP (textured soy protein)
2 Tbsp.. masa flour (optional)

Drain and rinse beans. Heat olive oil in large pot over medium-low heat. Add beans, chili powder, cumin, allspice and garlic. Stir gently to coat and warm over heat, stirring a few times, a few minutes until fragrant. Add Jose's Famous Salsa, broth and TSP. Bring to a boil, then simmer over low heat for at least 90 minutes. Add water one cup at a time if chili becomes too thick during cooking.

If you desire a slightly thicker and creamier chili, mix 2 Tbsp.. masa flour with water to form a thin paste. Add to chili during the final few minutes of cooking and stir well.

MARK OZIAS AND LISA BOULWARE moved to Sequim in 2004 to open a nursery.

After several years selling plants and produce at The Sequim Open Aire Market, Lisa and Mark opened The Red Rooster Grocery in downtown Sequim in April 2010.

Their goal at The Red Rooster Grocery is to highlight local food and Olympic Peninsula food producers, and Jose's Famous Salsa Chili is a fun example of the myriad food products that make our area special.

"Using Jose's Famous Salsa as your base makes this recipe extra easy (no prep work!) and extra delicious."

Lobster Potage

Submitted by Patti J. Mower

1 large lobster,
  shelled and chunked/sliced
  (save the shells for the stock)
1 small carrot
1 medium onion
8 tablespoons butter
Small handful of parsley
1/2 bay leaf
pinch of thyme
1/4 to 1/2 cup of brandy
1/2 cup dry white wine
1 cup water mixed with
  lobster & chicken stock
1 tablespoon sherry
3 cups milk
1/4 to 1/2 cup heavy cream
3 cups water
1/2 cup flour

Peel and dice carrot, peel and chop the onion very fine.
Heat 2 tablespoons of the butter in a skillet and sauté
the vegetables to a golden brown. Remove from skillet
and set aside. Add the parsley, bay leaf, and thyme
over the vegetables. Melt 2 more tablespoons of butter
in the same skillet and cook the lobster until it reddens,
shaking the pan once or twice . Spoon 1/4 cup brandy
over the lobster pieces and set aflame. Stir in the wine
and stock and allow the lobster to simmer, covered
for about 20 minutes.

Remove from heat and set aside.

"Great with dry champagne."

Bring milk and water to a boil. In a large saucepan, make a roux from butter and flour. When the mixture turns golden, stir in the hot milk and water mixture, and continue to stir until the mixture thickens. Add sautéed vegetables and lobster, stock and wine. Cover and simmer over low heat, stirring frequently, for 1-1/2 hours.

Remove any scum, add more milk if the mixture is not creamy enough. Return to low heat and stir in the heavy cream. If wanting a richer lobster color, add a drop or two of red food coloring. Adjust seasoning with salt and pepper. Stir in brandy to your choice of flavor just before serving.

For 15 years, I have been serving this at very special occasions ... most decadent. Great with dry champagne (try French or Italian).

Cold
Crab Soup

Submitted by Patti J. Mower

3 1/2 cups V-8 (or generic) vegetable juice
1 full cup frozen corn
3 medium or 2 large tomatoes fresh diced
      (may substitute canned, but not as good)
1 large cucumber, diced
1 medium green pepper, diced
1 cup red onion chopped
      (only red onion will work right)
1/4 cup parsley, chopped
1/4 cup fresh cilantro, chopped
3 Tbsp.. olive oil
2 cloves garlic, chopped
Hot pepper to taste ... optional
Salt and pepper to taste
1 to 2 cups cold cooked crab meat
6 to 8 large already cooked frozen or cold prawns

Pour vegetable juice into a ready-to-serve chilled bowl.
Add frozen corn, tomatoes, cucumber, green pepper,
onion, parsley, cilantro, olive oil, garlic, oil, and
mix lightly. Refrigerate for 1 hour.

Add crab and prawns and stir lightly.
Let sit for 15 to 20 minutes and serve.
Add dashes of hot sauce as desired.

North Olympic Peninsula Gazpacho

Submitted by Patti J. Mower

Dice:
1 or 2 large seeded cucumbers
3 large ripe tomatoes
1/2 red pepper
1/2 green pepper
1/2 red onion
2 stalks celery
3 cloves garlic
1/2 medium-size roasted pasilla pepper
       or a couple of roasted jalpenos
Cilantro (save some for garnish)

Set the pasilla and garlic aside.
Add the rest to:
4 cups V-8 juice
The juice of a large juicy lime
1/4 cup red wine vinegar
As much of your favorite hot sauce as you like
Salt and Pepper

Puree about 1/3 of the mixture plus all of the pasilla and garlic and add it back to the chunky 2/3.

Refrigerate and enjoy with some good homemade tortilla chips and a refreshing beverage.

Patti's Olympic Peninsula Red Chowder

Submitted by Patti J. Mower

As printed in the *Sequim Gazette*
(1st place winner 1992 Northwest Pacific
Clam Chowder Cook-off and 1st place winner
1993 Shelton Oyster State/Seafood Cook-off)

2 large cans crushed pear tomatoes
1 large Walla Walla onion, chopped
1 large green pepper, coarsely chopped
7 to 9 large Russet potatoes, peeled and cubed
2 pints chopped clams
1 cup flaked crabmeat
2 large stalks celery, sliced thin
Small bunch parsley, chopped
5 slices fried bacon, crushed
3 to 6 drops Red Hot Cayenne Sauce
1 tsp. thyme
Salt to taste (optional)

Using a Dutch oven, fry bacon and onion; add celery
and green pepper. Simmer on very low heat until
vegetables are hot, add crushed tomatoes, crab, clams,
and herbs. At the same time, boil large cubed potatoes
in water, drain almost all water and add all clam nectar
possible; boil until potatoes are almost soft. Add potatoes
to Dutch oven, add clams and crabmeat, heat at medium
temperature until almost boiling, stirring frequently,
turn down to simmer and cook 30-45 minutes.
Sprinkle parsley on top and serve (best the 2nd day).

Portuguese Sausage Soup

Submitted by Kathy Mahnerd

1 lb. spicy Italian sausage
1 cup sliced zucchini
1 cup chopped onion
1 cup sliced celery
1 cup California black olive wedges
3 large potatoes cut into 1/2 inch cubes
        or pasta (see below)
1 (1 lb. 12 oz.) can diced tomatoes, undrained
1 (15-1/4 oz.) can kidney beans, undrained
5 cups chicken broth
2 tsp. minced garlic
1/2 tsp. freshly ground black pepper
Chopped fresh basil (about 5 leaves)
Elbow macaroni (cook separately)
Parmesan cheese

Remove casings from sausages. Crumble meat
into Dutch oven (large pan) and sauté until cooked.
Drain off fat and rinse sausage in colander.
Add everything else to sausage in pan.
Bring to a boil and simmer, covered, 30 minutes,
or until all vegetables are tender.
Then add the cooked macaroni to the soup,
        if used instead of potato
Top with sprinkled parmesan cheese just before serving.
Makes 8 (2 cup) servings.

*Best the second or third day as flavors blend
        and soup will thicken.
*Cut down on the "heat" of soup by using mild sausage.

"Our friends and neighbors happily share the bounty of their gardens and endeavors on the Strait."

MOVING TO SEQUIM in 1997, after visiting for decades, has been a real treat to the senses in this world "where water is wealth." Our friends and neighbors happily share the bounty of their gardens and endeavors on the Strait.

We have helped pull crab pots, fished for Halibut and Salmon, picked all manner of berries, eaten all sorts of fruit and garden produce—and even pressed apples for cider.

We never realized there were pots with their own propane source to cook crabs outdoors, or that we would need new recipes for an abundance of food. The North Olympic Peninsula is a real land of plenty and the people here love to show others how they use the resources.

—Patsy and Dave Mattingly

Seafood Stew

Submitted by Patsy Mattingly

1/8 cup olive oil
1 1/2 cups chopped onion
3 cloves minced garlic
24 ounce can diced tomatoes in juice
1 1/2 cups sherry
8 ounces clam juice
1/3 cup tomato paste
2 cups water
2 bay leaves
1 tablespoon chopped fresh thyme
1 tablespoon fennel seeds, crushed
1/2 teaspoon dried crushed red pepper
10 clams, scrubbed
1 pound halibut filet cut in 2 inch pieces
1 pound salmon filet cut in 2 inch pieces
1/2 pound uncooked large shrimp
1/4 pound bay scallops
Fresh basil for garnish

Heat oil in heavy pot over medium heat. Add onions and garlic. Sauté until onions are tender. Add tomatoes, clam juice, tomato paste, water, sherry, and spices. Reduce heat and simmer uncovered until liquid is slightly reduced, about 45 minutes. Add clams to pot. Cover pot until clams open, about 10 minutes. Add seafood and simmer until seafood is just cooked through, about 5 minutes. Season to taste with salt and pepper. Garnish bowls with basil. Serves 8.

Zucchini-Basil Soup

Submitted by Kathy Mahnerd

2 pounds zucchini, coarsely chopped
3/4 cup chopped onion
2 large garlic cloves, chopped
1/4 cup olive oil
1 tablespoon butter
1 teaspoon salt
3 cups chicken stock
1/3 cup white wine
1/3 cup packed basil leaves
1/4 cup heavy cream

Melt butter with oil, then add garlic and onion into a 3 to 4 quart heavy saucepan and cook over medium-low heat, stirring occasionally, until softened, about 5 minutes. Add chopped zucchini and salt and cook, stirring occasionally, 5 minutes. Add chicken stock and white wine, then simmer, partially covered, until tender, about 15 minutes.

Puree soup with basil and cream in 2 batches in a blender (use caution when blending hot liquids.)

Season soup with salt and pepper. Serve hot or cold.

**"We loved Sequim so much
that we bought property
on our fourth day here."**

Zucchini-Basil Soup.

ERIC WAS A CAPTAIN and instructor for Continental Airlines, living in Houston, Texas, when three different soon-to-retire captains were having their six month check rides. All three were planning on retiring to a city called Sequim in the state of Washington. Since Eric only had two years left before he arrived at the 60-years-old cutoff date for flying, we decided to check out Sequim. We had already bought lakefront property in Minnesota in anticipation of having two small homes. I did Internet research and decided it was worth a look. We loved Sequim so much that we bought property on our fourth day here. Eric retired a few months early, so we sold our house and everything in it and headed to Sequim. It was September 1, 2003. It was cold and drizzly the day we arrived. Having our doubts as to the sanity of this move, we woke up the next morning to bright sunshine temperatures in the high 60s, and deer about 10 feet from our front window. We were delighted and have never regretted the move.

—*Kathy Mahnerd,* Sequim

Main Dishes and Traditional Foods

Old Haynes cooking crab in Dungeness, Washington.
Carol Polhamus Collection,
Museum & Arts Center in the Sequim-Dungeness Valley.

Christmas Morning Casserole

Submitted by Karen Kuznek-Reese

3 cups frozen hash browns
or 1 package (6 oz.) hash brown mix
1/3 cup chopped onion
1/4 cup chopped green bell pepper
8 slices bacon, cooked and crumbled
       (I substitute little smokies)
1 can (8oz) whole kernel corn (drained)
1-1/2 cup shredded cheddar cheese (6 oz)
1 cup milk
5 eggs (beaten)
1/2 tsp. salt
Dash of ground red pepper (cayenne)
Paprika

Preheat oven to 350F. Spread potatoes in ungreased dish (12 x 7-1/2 x 2). Top with onion, bell pepper, bacon, corn, and cheese. Mix remaining ingredients and pour over cheese. Sprinkle with paprika. Bake 35-40 minutes.

EVERY CHRISTMAS EVE I would put together a casserole that could be put in the oven on Christmas morning. It would be cooking while we were opening our presents. My daughter, Alicia, would complain that we had this every year and it always had something in it that she didn't like. Each year, of course, it would change depending on her tastes for that particular year.

When she was older, I was really surprised when she asked if I was making the casserole. It was a memory of hers and became a tradition to have this breakfast on Christmas morning. She also now eats everything that is included in that dish.

Christmas in 1996 in our living room
when Alicia was ten years old.

Corned Beef Hash with Eggs

Submitted by Vickie L. Johnson-Carroll

3 T butter
1 medium onion, finely chopped (about 1 cup)
2 cups small pieces cooked corned beef
2 to 3 cups sliced cooked potatoes
4 eggs

Heat butter in a large skillet (preferably cast iron) on medium heat. Add onion and cook until translucent. Mix in the pieces of corned beef and sliced potatoes. Spread out evenly in the pan. Increase heat to medium-high and press down on the mixture with a spatula. Brown the corned beef and potatoes. When browned, flip over in the pan so they brown on the other side. Press down again with the spatula. Add a little more butter to the pan if needed. Continue to cook until potatoes and the corned beef are browned. One at a time, break eggs into cup and slip into skillet on top of hash. Cover skillet and cook about 6 minutes or until eggs are set. Remove from heat. Serves 4.

Corned beef
hash with eggs

GROWING UP IN JAMESTOWN was wonderful! We knew everyone who lived down there, played with them, grew up with them. We swam in the straits, went clam digging, watched Dad dig geoduck, and my

My Parents: Harold and Hanna Johnson, 1949

Uncle Brick catch crab. My Dad (Harold "Bud" Johnson) had a dairy farm and he loved it. My brother Steve and I helped out so much on the farm, from herding the cows, to cleaning the milk tank, to haying. At times a special treat was going to The Creamery for ice cream. Dad also worked at Merrill & Ring for many years. Mom worked as a housekeeper for many years and cared for our family of six kids. Some of our meals consisted of anything from banana pancakes to oatmeal, to corned beef hash with eggs on top, and at times duck, venison, geoduck, clams, crab, devil fish, and salmon. Sometimes we would take a drive and pick up some shrimp. Sometimes Mom would fix her famous cinnamon rolls or homemade dinner rolls.

Crab Tacos

Submitted by Patti J. Mower

1/2 to 1 lb. crab meat, shucked
1/2 to 1 package taco seasoning
2/3 cup chopped green cabbage
1/3 cup chopped lettuces (mixed)
1/2 tomato, chopped big chunks
Olive oil, big splashes
1 medium bunch *fresh* cilantro, sliced
Pickled red onions (see recipe below)
1 whole lime, sliced and juiced, squeezed into mixture

Mix wet ingredients together, then add the crab and toss gently, not to break up the chunks. Take homemade or store-bought taco shells and pile on the crab mixture. Top with pickled red onions, maybe a dash of red hot. Enjoy warm or cold.

Pickled Red Onions

1/2 red onion, sliced thin
1/2 cup olive oil
1/2 fresh orange juice
Black pepper
1/4 generous teaspoon allspice powder
1/4 teaspoon oregano
4 tablespoons red wine vinegar
1/2 teaspoon sugar
Mix altogether and microwave for 2 minutes
and let sit in fridge for at least 20 minutes

PATTI AND DAVE MOWER and their son Matt
moved to Forks in 1987. Dave worked as a lineman
for the Clallam County PUD. When a position opened
in Sequim (which was their goal to begin with),
the Mowers moved to the Solmar development,
then purchased a home near town a couple of years
later. Matt graduated from Sequim High School with
honors in 2001. He graduated with a Bachelor's degree
in Science from Western with top honors and is now
finishing his PhD in Physics at MIZZOU in Missouri.

Patti has always loved to cook and has catered many
holiday parties for local physicians and customers who
came to know her from the pharmacies where she
worked as a pharmacy technician.

Patti won First Place in the Rotary Clam Chowder
Cookoff in 1992, and also in 1996 second and third place
for chowder and appetizers. She won Gold and Bronze
awards at the West Coast Oyster Shucking cookoffs,
also for chowder and appetizers.

DUNGENESS BARNHOUSE BED AND BREAKFAST. Originally from Ireland, Arthur and Minnie Rogers bought thirteen acres of Marine Drive waterfront property in 1924, built this barn and started a dairy farm. Over the years, the property was sold and divided. In 1959, an architect from New Jersey started the conversion from barn to house. The property was sold to the Nelsons in 1963, who completed the conversion. In the fall of 2003, the Wardens came to Sequim as Boeing retirees, bought the property and undertook the major renovations needed for the

almost 90 year old barn. An avid gardener and artist, Berta Warden moved over 100 roses from her former home, restored Fran Nelson's beautiful lilac garden, and added her own vision to the unique home and gardens. In 2010 the former dairy barn took on a new life as the *Dungeness Barnhouse Bed and Breakfast*. It has quickly become known for beautiful waterfront and garden views, warm hospitality and outstanding breakfasts. The *Dungeness Crab Portobello Benedict* (please see pages 62-63) has become a signature dish enjoyed by visitors to the Olympic Peninsula.

Dungeness Crab and Portobello Mushroom Benedict

Submitted by Berta Warden
Dungeness Barnhouse Bed & Breakfast

Serves 4:

1/2 cup Hollandaise Sauce
      (see page 30 for No Fail Blender Hollandaise)
4 eggs (poached)
4 Portobello mushrooms (gills and stems removed)
Meat from one large Dungeness crab
      (I always use fresh local crab)
1 tablespoon olive oil
1 clove garlic (finely diced)
2 ten-ounce bags of cleaned baby spinach
1 teaspoon fresh lemon juice
1 teaspoon fresh lemon zest
Pinch nutmeg
Pinch salt
1/4 teaspoon pepper

Preheat oven to 425 degrees

Place cleaned mushroom caps on lightly oiled baking sheet. Bake mushrooms for 10-12 minutes or until just tender. Remove mushrooms from oven and set aside.

Over medium heat in a small sauté pan or wok, add the olive oil, garlic, and spinach—tossing until slightly wilted. Add lemon juice, lemon zest, and nutmeg.

Dungeness Crab Portobello Mushroom Benedict
as served at the Dungeness Barnhouse Bed and Breakfast.

Poach 4 eggs in poaching cups until white is done
and yolks are still a little runny.

To serve:
Layer mushroom on the bottom, place 1/4 of spinach
atop mushroom, make a nest of Dungeness crab on top
of the spinach to cradle the egg, place poached egg in
nest and drizzle with Hollandaise sauce (see page 30).

E's Tater Tot Casserole

Submitted by Eric Adams
"Wee Mee Alth"
Jamestown, Washington

Tater Tot Casserole.
(Not my dish, but sure looks the same.)

Ingredients:

1 lb. Ground beef
2 cans Cream of Mushroom Soup
1 can Green Beans
Seasoning Salt
Shredded Cheddar Cheese
Mozzarella Cheese (if desired)
Tater Tots (or grocery store brand)

Directions:

- Preheat oven to 375F.
- Brown ground beef. Drain. Place in a bowl for mixing.
- Mix 1/4 cup Shredded Mozzarella Cheese
      with all other ingredients, except Tater Tots.
- Spread into a 2 quart casserole dish.
      Layer with Tater Tots.
- Top with your desired amount of Seasoning Salt
      and Shredded Cheddar Cheese.
- Cook for an hour. Pepper to taste.

A LITTLE BIT OF MY STORY and I'm sticking to it:
My sister cooked dinner for us when I was babysitting
my niece. How easy it was to make and how it tastes
was what caught me. When I started cooking a lot more
in my homestead, I started to make it almost twice
a week. Sometimes even more. It doesn't ever last long.

I've cooked it a couple times for the staff I work with
and a couple meetings. It didn't last long and the recipe
was requested by many. Very popular in my family.
There have been a couple modifications that are just
as good.

I like to call it "My Ghetto Lick" too! I take recipes and
always modify my way—and others' as well.

Fried Halibut Cheeks

by Walt Kardonsky
Submitted by Celeste Kardonsky Dybeck

One ten pound box of Alaska Halibut Cheeks
Or halibut meat cut into 3 inch squares
Flour
One beaten egg in a pie pan
1/2 mixture of flour and cornmeal, enough to coat fish.
Another pie pan works great for coating
salt and pepper
the flour cornmeal mixture
vegetable oil

Walt lands
a big one!

Walt and Dee Kardonsky.

Dredge halibut pieces in flour
Dip fish pieces in egg
Dredge a second time in flour/cornmeal mix

Fry pieces of coated Halibut in vegetable oil for about 3 minutes on each side. Coating will be a golden brown. Place "done" pieces in a warm oven while the rest of the halibut is being fried. Serve immediately with Walt's Tartar Sauce (recipe on page 31)

LIVING IN SEQUIM, Dad the tugboat captain worked out of Seattle for Foss Tug. Dad's tugboat days took him to Alaska. It was nothing for Dad to arrive at home with a ten pound box of halibut cheeks under his arm. The entire family would gather round to admire the halibut. Dad would spend hours, at least it seemed like it, grating onions, eggs and pickles for his tartar sauce. Once finished he would proudly place the heaped bowl in the refrigerator. About an hour before dinner, dad would start frying his cheeks. Yes, all ten pounds. Our family would devour that entire box in one meal. We would heap the tartar sauce on the halibut. It was delicious!

Gail's Crab Cakes

Submitted by R.G. "Rick" Godfrey

2 cups fresh Dungeness crab meat
1 cup plain bread crumbs
1/2 cup finely minced celery
1/2 to 3/4 cup finely minced onion
1 green or red bell pepper, chopped
2 teaspoons dry mustard
3/4 teaspoons tabasco
1 large egg
1/4 cup mayonnaise
1 tablespoon lemon juice
3/4 teaspoon Worcestershire sauce
Additional bread crumbs for coating the crab cakes
        before frying.
Half cup or more vegetable oil for frying.
Makes 12-plus cakes.
Do not break crab up too much when mixing the cakes.

GAIL STONE DELORM was born in the Port Angeles
Hospital in 1938 and came home to the farm house
on Port Williams Road. She joined her sister Margie
(Margaret); later brother Gregg joined the family.

She went to school in the eight-room school in Sequim,
which didn't have kindergarten so at age five she went
into first grade. Living on the farm was a treasured way
of life. Gail loved being out with the workers, driving the
silage truck and tractors pulling the trailers with baled
hay. At the age of five she drove her Uncle George's
army jeep, which pulled the fork to release the loose
hay in the barn below Medsker Road (now gone).

She married in 1958 to Bob DeLorm. He spent three
years in the Army then became a Washington State

"Living on the farm was a treasured way of life."

Trooper in 1964. They lived in Wenatchee where their daughter Tracy was born, and then transferred to Ellensburg where their son Robert Gregg was born in 1969. In 1972 Bob was transferred to Sequim. Bob died in 1993.

In 1974, when Bob and Bette Duncan remodeled the old Dungeness Creamery into the Dungeness Tavern, Gail's sister's husband Perry Elliott opened the Bandits Pizza Parlor in the tavern. Bandits was there for one year

continued on next page ...

The Stone Kids.

Crab Cakes.

before moving uptown where the *101 Diner* is currently located, where it remained until 1989. Father, Stacy Stone, died in May 1995 and Mother in 2003. Gail's older sister Margie also died in 2003.

ONE STORY I LOVE to tell, which gives us the memory as to how small Sequim was at one time, is when our barn burned down in 1948. Then you had to dial up the operator. My Aunt Mildred Godfrey dialed up the operator and wanted to call 444 which was our number on the farm. The operator told Aunt Mildred that Margaret probably wouldn't answer because their barn was burning.

The beach in Dungeness where I have lived for 40 years now has brought us the many food treasures of Dungeness crab, clams, geoduck and salmon. I enjoy fishing the salt water probably the most. Son Bob is a fisheries technician for the Jamestown S'Klallam Tribe. His wife Lori is a Natural Resources Technician. Daughter Tracy Venegas is a Special Education teacher at Helen Haller Elementary School.   — *R.G. Godfrey*

On the Beach Seafood Pot

Submitted by Lyle and Vena Isert

1 to 2 cleaned crabs divided into sections,
    legs and body attached
1 to 2 lbs. steamer clams
1 to 2 lbs. mussels
12 to 15 large prawns, deveined
4 large stalks of celery, sliced
4-6 green onions, sliced
3 large garlic cloves, crushed or sliced thin
2 to 3 cubes butter
2 cups white wine or 1 bottle lager beer
    (enough to cover all seasoning)
Either 1 bag of Zatarain's New Orleans Shrimp
    & Crab Boil or 1 heaping tablespoon of Pike Place
    Northwest Clam & Mussel Seasoning (ask for it
    at your seafood counter at the market)
1 to 2 lemons cut into quarters or sliced
Dashes of hot sauce to taste
Small handful of chopped parsley

Place all ingredients in kettle. Steam or hot simmer
until shells open, about 10-15 minutes (don't over-
or undercook). Spoon broth over seafood and serve
with crunchy fresh warm French bread. Make sure you
have larger bowls so everyone can have lots of broth.
Yum!

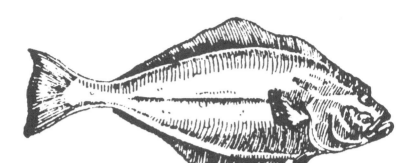

Halibut Oscar

Submitted by Patti J. Mower

2 pounds halibut filet (don't cut)
1 large or 2 small Dungeness crabs, shelled
1 large stalk celery, sliced thin
1 small green onion, sliced
1 garlic clove or shallot, chopped or minced
2 three-ounce packages cream cheese
1/3 cup mayonnaise
1/3 cup cheddar and Monterey cheese, grated
1/4 cup Parmesan cheese, grated fine
4 ounces white wine
1/2 to 3/4 cup bread crumbs

In a large bowl combine the crab, celery, onion, garlic or shallot, cream cheese, mayonnaise, cheddar and Monterey, and half of the wine. Grease baking dish with ample butter and place the halibut skin side down in pan (remove skin beforehand). Pour over the rest of the wine. Spread the cheese mixture over top of fish, using every bit. Sprinkle on the Parmesan and top with bread crumbs. Place in preheated 325 degree oven and cover with foil for the first 20 minutes. Remove foil and bake for an additional 15 minutes. The fish should not be opaque, but white and solid, the topping bubbly and the bread crumbs browned.

Mexican Lasagna

Submitted by Patti J. Mower

1 lb. ground beef
1/3 lb. chorizo (optional)
1-2 packages taco seasoning
1-2 cans chili or black beans (drained)
1/2 cup chopped white sweet onion
1/2 can large olives, sliced
1 medium can tomato sauce
1 bottle (16 oz.) chunky salsa
1 clove garlic, chopped
1 batch fresh cilantro, chopped
Dashes of Chipotle Tabasco sauce (optional)
4 oz. cream cheese
1 full cup medium to sharp grated cheddar cheese
1/2 cup Cotija cheese, chunked
1/2 cup grated mixture of Parmesan, Asiago
          and Romano cheeses
1/2 package ribbed lasagna

Brown the ground meats, add onion and as much taco
seasoning as desired. Next add the tomato sauce, salsa,
olives, garlic, and a few drops of the Chipotle Tabasco
sauce. Stir and simmer. It will smell wonderful.
Meanwhile, take the grated cheeses and mix with the
cream cheese and cilantro. Set aside. Cook lasagna until
al dente and drain. Layer your lasagna dish with pasta,
then meat sauce mixture, then the cheese mixture
(by blobs). Finish with a layer of the beans, and repeat.
You should end up with three layers. Sprinkle with all
remaining cheeses and more seasoning if preferred.
Bake at 375 degrees for 45-50 minutes until cheeses are
browned and sauce is bubbling. Enjoy with Chianti or
a margarita. Don't forget the salad and chips and salsa!

Old Italian Bianco Lasagna

Submitted by Patti J. Mower

Preheat oven to 350F.
1 bunch fresh asparagus
1 can quartered artichoke hearts
3/4 to 1 lb. Black Forest ham, sliced thin
3 to 4 grilled chicken breasts, chunked or sliced
4 oz. cream cheese
8 oz. 4% cottage cheese or Ricotta
1 package sliced Provolone
1 cup shredded Mozzarella
1 tub shredded 3 cheese Italian blend
      (Parmesan, Asiago, Romano)
1 can cream of asparagus soup
1 can cream of chicken/herb soup
1/2 glass of dry white wine (4-5 ounces)
1 box lasagna pasta (rippled edge)
1/2 can medium to large sliced black olives
1 cup sliced fresh mushrooms
Medium sized handful of Italian seasoning
Handful of sliced fresh green onion
Handful of fresh or dried parsley

Steam the asparagus slightly and set aside. In a mixing bowl, take your hands and mix the cheeses and some of the parsley until thoroughly blended; set aside. Next, put the soup (undiluted) with the wine, Italian seasoning, mushrooms, green onions and black olives on low heat in a "soup" pot and simmer. Cook the pasta until slightly limp but not done; drain.

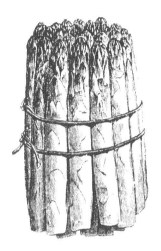

Rub your lasagna dish with olive oil and start your layers with the pasta. Next layer the ham, then chicken. Place the asparagus and artichokes evenly on top of the meat. Spoon and spread on the sauce, then the cheese mixture by small spoonfuls. Sprinkle with more shredded cheese and top with the Provolone.

Start over again until you have 3 to 4 layers. Top with any leftover cheeses. Place in oven and cook for two hours or until golden brown and bubbling.

*Cook's Note: I created this recipe in 2008 after having *Chicken Asparagus Involtini* at Chestnut Cottage in Port Angeles.

Traditional Lasagna

Submitted by Patti J. Mower

Feeds 4-6

1 lb. ground beef
1/3 cup sliced pepperoni
1/3 cup sliced salami
1/3 lb. ground Italian sausage
1 full cup fresh sliced mushrooms
1/2 cup sliced black olives
1/4 chopped fresh sweet white onion
1 jar of your favorite marinara sauce (24 oz.)
1-2 teaspoons dried Italian or Greek seasoning
          (e.g., Penzeys)
1/2 cup red wine
1 clove garlic, chopped
1 handful fresh spinach leaves and sliced zucchini
          (optional)
4 oz. cream cheese
1 to 2 cups shredded Romano, Parmesan, Asiago (mixed)
1 to 2 cups shredded mozzarella
1 bunch fresh parsley, chopped (or small handful dried)
2/3 cup ricotta or 4% small curd cottage cheese
1/2 box ribbed lasagna pasta

Start by cooking the ground beef, pepperoni, salami,
Italian sausage, onion and seasoning until browned.
Drain if necessary. Add mushrooms and olives and cook
for another 5-7 minutes. Mushrooms will be brown and
easy to work into the meat mixture. Add marinara and
wine; stir and let simmer. Meanwhile, start a large pot
of water boiling. Add salt and olive oil. Now add the pasta
and cook until not completely al dente; drain and let
sit until cooled (warm). In a medium to large mixing
bowl put in the cream cheese, cottage cheese or ricotta,

a full handful of all the mixed dry cheeses and parsley. Take your hands and get right in there mixing all until well blended. Taste a bit off your finger; yum.

In your lasagna dish, place in a layer of pasta, add meat marinara mixture and spread. (If using spinach and/or zucchini, place on top.) Next, by tablespoonfuls, put on the ricotta/cream cheese mixture in 5-7 blobs per layer. Do not spread. Then sprinkle with loose cheeses. Repeat.

You should end up with three layers. Place in a 375F oven (you might want to put aluminum foil or a cooking sheet underneath, depending on the depth of your baking dish). Bake for 50 minutes or until cheese on top is golden brown and sauce is bubbling. Enjoy with a great green salad and mellow red wine.

Stuffed Steamer Clams

Submitted by Patti J. Mower

As printed in a "Kitchen Korner" article by Marian Platt in the *Sequim Gazette:*

TO PATTI J. MOWER, clams and the fall go together. Having been raised with the beach and the bay as her front yard by Lummi Island, and having a father who was a commercial fisherman in the summer, she had great opportunities to develop delicious seafood dishes. Here's a real winner—took 2nd place at Shelton Oyster/State Seafood Cook-off in 1992.

In a shallow baking dish pour 2/3 c dry white wine. Combine 4 oz. cream cheese, 1/2 c sharp cheddar cheese, grated, 1/2 c minced celery, 1/2 c minced onion, several dashes Red Hot Cayenne Sauce,

continued on next page ...

1/2 c chopped zucchini, 3/4 c mozzarella cheese, grated, 1 T minced cilantro and 1/4 c chopped parsley and mix very thoroughly; let stand 10 minutes. Steam 2 lbs. clams until opened; cool slightly. Discard any that do not "pop open." Stuff each clam with a heaping teaspoonful of mixture and place in a single layer on baking sheet and bake for 10 minutes in a 350F oven. Remove from oven and generously sprinkle with Parmesan cheese and Italian bread crumbs; broil until golden and serve immediately.

Patti's Chianti Smoked Sockeye

Submitted by Patti J. Mower

1/2 cup sea salt or non-iodized salt
4 to 6 cups Chianti or dark red wine,
      not boxed or cheap; must be dry
      (best bet: Livingston Chianti, larger bottle)
1-1/2 cups dark brown sugar
2 cups water to finish covering the salmon
      for the brining period
2 tablespoons garlic powder
1/2 cup low salt soy sauce
Either dashes of cayenne sauce
      or a tablespoon of cayenne powder

Mix all ingredients until dissolved to make a brine. Let sit for a half-hour at a cool temperature. Taste and add additional salt or spice if desired.

Place clean, slime-free and dry 4 to 6 inch sections of salmon filet in a large stainless or glass container. Add enough brine to cover well. Now soak for 12 hours in a very cool place. Remove and pat dry; do not rinse. Place on wire racks and leave exposed to cool free air for 8-10 hours to become pellucid (the fish will shine). Cover with cheese cloth if you prefer.

Smoke over alder chips (no other wood substitution will do) at 225F for 1 hour 45 minutes to 2 hours, for a dark solid smoked salmon. Remove from smoker and place on wire racks again until cool. The fish will continue cooking until cool so don't let it cook to your liking in the smoker or it will become overdone.

Gently pull off skin and remove grey fat layers as they leave a metallic taste in the mouth. You want to save just the moist smoky meat. Very easy to vacuum pack. Use minimal vacuum just to get the air out or the fish will turn rubbery. Remember to not smoke little pieces or a whole side.

Irish Dinner

Submitted by Patti J. Mower

IRISH LAYERED POTATOES (prepared like lasagna)
5-6 medium/large russet potatoes
2-3 medium/large leeks
1 cup/pint cream or half-n-half
1 block sharp "white" cheddar cheese
1 lb. butter (for greasing dish and between layers)

continued on next page ...

2-3 shallots or fresh green onions
Pinch of thyme

Grease large glass/ceramic casserole dish. Grate cheddar
cheese. Slice leeks into thin circles. Slice/chop
shallots or green onions. Slice potatoes with skin left on.
Cut 1 cube butter into chunks. Layering: 1st layer
with sliced potatoes; 2nd layer leeks and small chunks
of butter; 3rd layer white cheddar; 4th layer shallots or
onions with pinch of thyme. Pour over with cream.
Continue for 3-4 layers. Bake at 325 degrees for 20-30
minutes and top with grated cheddar. Continue baking
until bubbly and brown, approximately 45 minutes.

IRISH MARINATED STEAKS

A rich wonderful way with steaks, Irish style.

3 to 4 New York or Sirloin steaks
1 pint Irish stout or Guinness
         (as long as it's a heavier Irish beer)
5-6 shallots, coarsely chopped
1 cube butter

Mix together the stout, shallots and butter while
while warming over low heat. Set aside until slightly
warmer than room temperature. Place steaks in this
marinade and refrigerate for at least 2-3 hours.
Then either pan fry in a well greased pan (such as
bacon grease), or better still—grill them over good
apple or alder chips.

Options: Top with fried onions, or also marinate
some fresh large sliced mushrooms to put on top.
Think Irish. Something green? We've also added
Irish whiskey to the marinade just before cooking.

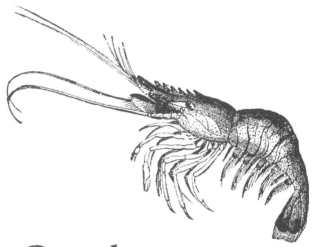

Shrimp Bread

Submitted by Mayme Faulk
on behalf of the Soroptomist International of Sequim

1 cup mayonnaise
1/2 cup sour cream
1 tbsp. Beau Monde seasoning
4 tbsp. chopped green onions
1 1/2 cups grated cheddar cheese
2 cups of salad shrimp
2 loaves french bread, split in half lengthwise
Mix together the first 5 ingredients.
Spread 1/2 cup of mixture on each half loaf of bread.
Spread 1/2 cup cooked shrimp meat on each half loaf.
Bake at 450F for 5 - 7 minutes.
Cut into quarters and serve.

Margaret & Stacy Stone.

Margaret's
Round Steak Casserole

Submitted by R.G. Rick Godfrey

2 lbs. round steak, cut into 1/2 inch cubes
2 tablespoons oil
1 1/2 cups chopped onion
2 tablespoons flour
1/2 cup diced celery
1 teaspoon salt
1/4 teaspoon Worcestershire sauce
1 can tomato sauce
1 can sliced mushrooms
1 cup sour cream

Stone Family Farm

In a large fry pan, brown meat well in oil. Add onion, garlic, cook until limp but not brown. Stir in flour, add celery, tomato sauce, mushrooms and liquids (sour cream, Worcestershire), salt and pepper. Mix thoroughly. Turn into a greased 2 quart casserole dish. Bake uncovered in a slow oven (300 degrees) for one and a half hours or until meat is tender. Serve over noodles or rice.

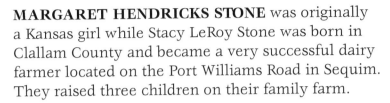

MARGARET HENDRICKS STONE was originally a Kansas girl while Stacy LeRoy Stone was born in Clallam County and became a very successful dairy farmer located on the Port Williams Road in Sequim. They raised three children on their family farm.

Margaret enjoyed genealogy as a hobby when she was not playing bridge. Stacy was an Irrigation Festival Grand Pioneer and Margaret served as the Honorary Grand Pioneer in 1989.

Stacy was very active in the management of the Sequim Co-op as well as the Dungeness Valley water supply. He also served on the board of directors for the Western Farmers Association (WFA), the Sequim schools, and the Sequim Bank. The Stones enjoyed fishing, clamming and boating on the Strait of Juan de Fuca islands and waters from Dungeness to Neah Bay. During the summer months they made several packing trips on horseback into the Olympic Mountains.

Margaret (left) with her three children,
Gregg, Gail, and Margie,
and her sister Mildred H. Godfrey (far right),
before diving into the chocolate pie!

Mildred's Chicken Breast Supreme

Submitted by R.G. "Rick" Godfrey

Serves 6 persons

3 chicken breasts
      cut in half lengthwise
1/4 teaspoon paprika
1 chicken bouillon cube
1 cup boiling water
1/4 cup white wine
1/2 teaspoon curry powder
1/2 teaspoon instant minced onion
Pepper to taste
Mushroom sauce
      to cover and taste (recipe below)

Sprinkle chicken with seasoned salt and paprika. Place in 11 x 7 x 1 baking dish. Dissolve bouillon cube in boiling water, then add wine, onion, curry powder and pepper. Pour over chicken. Cover with foil and bake at 350F for 50 minutes. Uncover and bake 45 minutes longer or until tender. Remove chicken to serving platter.

Reserve pan juices and prepare mushroom sauce. Make up white sauce (2 tablespoons butter, 2 tablespoons all-purpose flour, 1 cup milk). In small saucepan over medium heat, melt butter, add flour and stir until butter and flour are well combined. Pour in milk, stirring constantly as it thickens. When thickened, add 1 cup drained canned mushrooms and serve over chicken.

Mildred and George Godfrey.

MILDRED HENDRICKS was born in Kansas and George Ritchie Godfrey was a native of Clallam County. Mildred taught in the Blue Mountain School in her early years, living with local families during the winter months.

George bought his father's hardware store (Godfrey's) on Washington Street in Sequim, managed it for many years, and was project manager for such building projects as the Graysmarsh Farm Homestead.

The Godfreys built their own first house on the corner of Second Avenue and Maple Street; it still stands there today. Besides raising four sons they were avid skiers, hunters, fishermen, bridge players and golfers.

Godfrey home
(1936 photo)

Godfrey's
Hardware Store

Gramma Dee's Crab Casserole

Submitted by Celeste Kardonsky Dybeck

6 slices of bread, diced
2 to 3 cups crab meat
1 onion, chopped
1 to 1-1/2 cups celery, chopped
3 cups 2% milk (non-fat doesn't hold up as well)
6 eggs (about)
3/4 cup mayonnaise
2 cups grated cheese

Mix bread, crab, onion, celery in a large bowl.
Pour into large (9 x 12) greased casserole dish.

Beat eggs, add milk and mayo. Beat together until
thoroughly mixed. Pour over crab mixture. If the egg
and milk mixture doesn't cover the casserole stuff
add more.

Refrigerate overnight.
Remove from refrigerator about 1 to 2 hours
before you put it in the oven.

Bake at 325 degrees for about 1 to 1-1/2 hours.

Spread the grated cheese on top for the
last 15 minutes of baking.

A great side dish for Holiday dinners,
Thanksgiving and Christmas.

Enjoy!

DEE KARDONSKY moved from North Dakota to Sequim during her high school years. She was in the Sequim Class of 1949. Dad was born in Port Angeles in 1926. Dee and Walt had seven kids, all raised in Sequim. The family home was a block from the Sequim School and the place was always rocking with activity and hordes of people. Grampa Swanberg, who was confined to his wheelchair, also lived with us.

Dee-Doe started making her Crab Casserole side dish in the early 1960's. Not a holiday would go by without mom making "crab casserole." The seven Kardonsky kids all loved it. Once the kids grew up and left home, Mom would hit the road and take her yummy crab casserole with her. Always a hit with family and seldom any leftovers. Siblings continue to make Mom's crab casserole. She used to spoon a can of cream of mushroom soup on the top before adding the cheese. We all "ditched" that idea, because it detracted from the crab. Recently, for brother Tim's birthday potluck, I offered to bake a cake, and Candy's quick response was, "No, bring Mom's crab casserole." It is still a hit.

Kardonsky Family Members.

Mrs. Ritchie's Hot Crab Soufflé

Submitted by Craig A. Ritchie

From the *Seattle Times* file, 1960

Makes 8 servings

8 slices bread
2 cups crab
1/2 cup mayonnaise
1 small onion, peeled and chopped
1 small green bell pepper, chopped
1 cup chopped celery
3 cups milk
4 eggs
1 can (10 3/4 ounces) mushroom soup
1 cup grated cheddar cheese
Paprika

Dice half of the bread into a baking dish. Mix the crab, mayonnaise, onion, green bell pepper and celery together and spread over the diced bread. Trim the crusts from the remaining 4 slices of bread and place over the crab mixture. Mix the milk and eggs together and pour over the mixture in the casserole. Cover and refrigerate overnight.

Bake in a preheated 325-degree oven for 15 minutes. Remove from the oven and spoon the soup over the top. Top with the cheese and sprinkle with the paprika. Bake for 1 hour longer and serve immediately.

IN 1954, when I was going into the 4th grade at Magnolia Elementary School in Seattle, in the class of Mrs. Linville (whom we thought, mistakenly, was the famous Wunda Wunda the clown: 1953-1972 King TV kids' show, *en.wikipedia.org/ wiki/Wunda Wunda*) my mom entered the Crab Soufflé recipe of her across-the-street neighbor Verna Knight in a national contest and won $500. We were famous! It turned out to be a good family recipe (although not really ours) and a great way to eat fresh-cooked Dungeness crab.

Seattle Woman Rates First In 11-City Contest

MRS. O. T. RITCHIE, Seattle, was the winner of the $500 national prize in a recipe contest sponsored by newspapers in 11 cities. It was announced by the Department of Home Economics at Ohio State University, Columbus, where the grand prize recipes from all cities were tested.

Mrs. Ritchie, whose hot crab souffle won the grand prize for her in the contest conducted by the Seattle Times, is a homemaker, a free lance writer and the mother of two sons.

Newspapers which conducted contests simultaneously with The Blade and the Seattle Times were the Columbus Dispatch, Denver Post, Allentown Call-Chronicle, Duluth News-Tribune, Houston Chronicle, Indianapolis Star and News, Spokane Spokesman-Review, Cincinnati Enquirer and Marion (Ind.) Chronicle. Here is the winning recipe.

HOT CRAB SOUFFLE

8 slices bread
2 c crab or shrimp
½ c mayonnaise
1 onion, chopped
1 green pepper, chopped
1 c celery, chopped
3 c milk
4 eggs
1 can mushroom soup
Grated cheese
Paprika

Dice half of bread into baking dish. Mix crab (or shrimp), mayonnaise, onion, green pepper and celery and spread over diced bread.

Trim crusts from remaining four slices and place trimmed slices over crab mixture. Mix eggs and milk together and pour over mixture. Place in refrigerator over night.

Bake in 325-degree oven for 15 minutes. Take from oven and pour soup over the top. Top with cheese and paprika. Bake 1 hour in 325-degree oven.

Yield: 12 servings.

MRS. O. T. RITCHIE

Seattle Times Article,

Nan's Crab-Stuffed Green Peppers

Submitted by R.G. "Rick" Godfrey

6 green bell peppers
2 cups cooked crab meat
1/4 cup of dry white wine
1 teaspoon lemon juice
1 cup light cream
1 cup cooked rice
4 tablespoons butter
2 tablespoons cornstarch
1 teaspoon salt
1/4 tsp. ground nutmeg
Paprika

Nan's Crab-stuffed Green Peppers.

Cut tops off all peppers, remove seeds. Parboil peppers five minutes; drain. Scald cream, add butter and nutmeg. Mix cornstarch, wine, lemon juice and salt. Add to cream. Cook until thickened, stirring constantly. Combine with crab meat and rice, and spoon into peppers. Sprinkle with paprika. Bake in a greased baking dish in a moderate oven (350) for 20 minutes. Serves 6.

NAN SHIRLEY was born in Breckenridge, Minnesota. Richard George Godfrey is a native of the Olympic Peninsula, born in Sequim. Nan is a graduate of Stephens College in Missouri and also the University of Minnesota. She taught elementary grades and art. Richard (Rick) is a University of Minnesota graduate and worked many years for the corporations of Honeywell and TRW. Rick still does management consulting for international corporations. Having lived all over the USA and Europe, they are very happily settled down in Sequim for retirement.

Golf, cards, cooking, hunting, fishing and travel are their main hobbies these days.

They have three children—Pamela, Eric and Greg—who visit them regularly during holidays and vacations. They still travel extensively and especially love Paris, France, where they have lived three different times. The Godfrey families are pioneers in both Sequim and Port Angeles.

Nan S. and Richard G. Godfrey.

Mom's Potato Pancakes

Submitted by Joanna Hays

3 Medium Potatoes Grated
2 eggs separated
    Whip the egg whites
    and add with egg yolks
    to the grated potatoes.
1 tsp. salt
1-1/2 tablespoons flour
1/2 tsp. baking powder

Joanna Kimler in front of
Bill's Plumbing on Bell Street.

Mix together and cook by spoonfuls in skillet in hot oil.
Cook on both sides until golden brown.

Excellent with applesauce or sliced peaches with juice!

I WAS LUCKY ENOUGH to spend most of my
childhood growing up in Sequim. In the early 60's my
parents bought an older building that housed a
creamery in the center of town where they relocated
their plumbing business from our little house.

We lived on the second story over the plumbing
business and each day after school would come home
and do our daily chores in the plumbing shop and
then retreat to our huge apartment just up the stairs.

My mom was a wonderful cook and was great at using
left-overs and being conscious of the family budget.
One of my favorite dinners was potato pancakes and
peaches. Everyone loved it when we had it for dinner;
it was almost like having breakfast. When available
we would have grandma's home-canned peaches but
when we were out we used store-bought canned ones.
Either way nice and sweet!

We didn't have a freezer but we had a huge pantry
and it was always well stocked with canned goods.
I remember every fall we would go out to the
Carlsborg Store and stock up on the canned goods
by the case to fill the pantry for winter. I have
wonderful memories of our family dinners each night
and everything we shared. I grew up in this small
town and watched it grow from dirt roads to paved
streets with other small business moving in. Today
we have a thriving downtown, so much more developed
than when I was a kid and we have an abundance
of fresh produce available. No more canned peas,
they were the worst.

Joanna Kimler with her cat and cat-eye glasses
in front of Bill's Plumbing in the sixties.

Stuff Casserole

Submitted by Renee Lemmon-Bleile

Preheat oven to 350 degrees

1 lb. hamburger
1/2 head cabbage, shredded
2 to 3 large potatoes, thinly sliced
2 to 3 carrots, shredded or grated
1 can cream of mushroom soup
6 to 8 slices of American cheese

Crumble 3/4 of the hamburger into a 9 x 13 pan.
Layer potatoes, cabbage and carrots. Salt and pepper
each layer. Crumble remainder of hamburger on carrots.
Spread soup on top and lay cheese on top of soup.

Cover with foil and bake for 1-1/2 hours;
uncover for the last 1/2 hour.

*"As with all our family gatherings,
a picnic lunch ensued, with lots
of laughter, chatting, games, running,
and memories being shared."*

THE LEMMON/CAYS FAMILIES always gathered on the weekend before Memorial Day to clean, mow, trim and generally clean up the areas around the family graves at the old Dungeness Cemetery. Even Eldon and Thelma, with their children, would come from Forks for this annual get-together.

As with all our family gatherings, a picnic lunch ensued, with lots of laughter, chatting, games, running, and memories being shared.

I sometimes hope our grandchildren will have a few little tidbits of memories of these growing-up years as I have had. My roots are here and always will be.

—Renee Lemmon Bleile, Sequim, Washington

From left: Miles D. Lemmon, Truman L. Lemmon (Renee's father), Eldon Lemmon, Chester Lemmon, Stella Lemmon Dodge, and Marie. Missing from the photograph is Ted Lemmon.

Tofu Burgers

Submitted by Genaveve Starr

Serves 4 to 6
> depending on how large you like your patties.

16 oz. Firm Tofu
> (Island Springs is my personal favorite brand)

2 large eggs
2 slices bread
> (whole grain or other quality sandwich bread)

1/4 cup minced shallot
1-1/2 tsp. minced garlic
1-1/2 tsp. Spike Salt-Free Seasoning
1/4 tsp. fresh ground black pepper
1 dash cayenne pepper
2 Tbsp.. butter
1 Tbsp.. vegetable oil

- Drain tofu and squeeze in a tea towel
  to remove excess water.
- Mince garlic and shallot. In a small pan,
  sauté on medium-low with 1 Tbsp.. butter,
  until shallots are translucent and soft.
- Crack eggs into a mixing bowl; beat with Spike,
  pepper, and cayenne.
- Crumble tofu, mix into eggs with fork.
- Tear bread into crumbs.
- Add sautéed onions and garlic to tofu mixture,
  mixing in with fork.
- Use hands to gently incorporate breadcrumbs into tofu
  mix. Texture should be similar to a meat burger.
- Form into patties.
- Heat oil in a frying pan on medium heat, add butter.
- Sauté patties until golden brown (approximately five
  minutes each side).

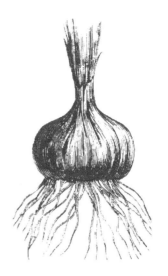

Tofu Burgers Can be served on buns with burger fixings, or on their own with your favorite sauce on top.

KARL STOKKE AND GENAVEVE STARR moved to Sequim in 1971, living at "Cassidy Creek," an old forty-acre dairy farm surrounded by state forest, with a creek and pond and a big barn.

Karl built a pottery studio and Genaveve pursued her passion for calligraphy. Over the years, Karl worked at a lumber mill and then for Sequim School District as custodian, retiring after 21 years in 2012.

Genaveve had a graphic design studio, worked for Community Action and Peninsula College, and volunteered in many community organizations.

Their daughter, Mara Stokke, grew up here and attended Sequim Schools. She graduated from the American Academy of Dramatic Arts and joined their theater group. She is currently working as a graphic artist and web developer.

Traditional Foods

Submitted by Rosie Zwanziger

ONE OF MY EARLIEST MEMORIES
is going with my grandmother, Ethel Wood
Johnson, to Port Williams at extreme
low tides when big rocks were exposed.
She would take along a sturdy stick to poke
around under the huge rocks in hopes of
pulling out an octopus. Any Jamestown kids
who happened to be about when the octopus
was cooked were treated to a leg—a chewy,
all day seafood sucker! And what a treat it
was, sucker and all.

My mother, Edith Johnson Cusack, dragged
all of her kids on frequent family outings that
almost always had something to do with food.
Mom always traveled prepared, with buckets
and at least one shovel in her trunk, ever
ready for low tides or prolific berry patches.
We dug clams, gathered oysters and mussels,
netted smelt, picked wild blackberries, black-
caps, huckleberries and salmon berries.
We ate steamers, pan fried butters, oysters
and smelt; clam chowder and oyster stew;
wild blackberry pies and berry jams galore.

Every once in a while we'd come across
soapberry bushes from which we'd gather
the berries and make "Indian ice cream."
I don't think any of us kids really cared much
for "swassom," but we humored Mom and
helped with the beating of the berries, as
this was a special dessert when she was a kid.

text continues on page 100

Iris Johnson tending salmon in Jamestown in the mid-1970s.

Mom's brothers, Brick (Harris), Muff (Wilfred), Bud (Harold) and Russell Johnson all crabbed, fished, and hunted ducks and pheasants and shared their bounty, so we generally had our fill of crab (plentiful back then) with the occasional halibut fillet, skate wing, geoduck or even a feathered duck thrown in for variety.

EVERY FALL, UNCLE BRICK smoked dozens of salmon in his huge walk-in smokehouse. It was done the traditional way and was hard smoked, what we called "Indian-smoked" salmon. It was hard, dry, smoky and salty, kind of like a jerky, and would keep for years. Aunt Irish would simmer it in water to reconstitute it for dinner. She also used to smoke horse clam necks, and there is nothing quite like them—a real delicacy. Boiled fish heads and salmon egg soup were some other meals we might be served at Aunt Iris and Uncle Brick's. Uncles Russell and Muff had a special fondness for duck soup, and it would often be simmering on the stove when we'd stop by.

In writing this, it occurs to me that many of my fondest memories of family, Jamestown, and childhood experiences involved traditional foods! To this day I relish the chance to dig clams, gather oysters and mussels, pick berries and prepare and share our traditional foods. I'm already looking forward to our annual Traditional Food Meal. Will someone bring smoked horse neck clams, please?

I know many long-time Sequimites will also have fond memories of the many salmon, clam and oyster bakes held on the Johnson Beach in Jamestown. For decades, Brick and Iris Johnson hosted these events as fundraisers for the Lion's Club, VFW, or Irrigation Festival.

—*Rosie Zwanziger (Johnson and Wood families)*

Grilled Veal Chops

Submitted by Eric Mahnerd

2 (14 – 16 oz.) veal chops
Garlic salt
Lemon pepper
Cracked pepper

Marinade:
3 Tbsp. extra virgin olive oil
1 Tbsp. red wine vinegar
1 Tbsp. fresh lemon juice
2 tsp. dried basil
   or
3 Tbsp. fresh basil,
   snipped into small pieces
1 tsp. chopped
   dehydrated onions
1/2 tsp. capers
1/2 tsp. cracked pepper
1/2 tsp. sea salt
1/2 tsp. garlic salt

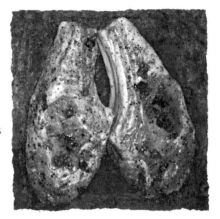

Veal Chops in Marinade.

Preparation:
Sprinkle chops with garlic salt,
   lemon pepper and cracked pepper.
Place all ingredients for marinade in a 9 x 9 glass
   baking dish and then mash capers.
Leave chops in marinade for two hours, at room
   temperature, turning every 20 minutes or so.
Cook on grill until medium, about 135F on an instant
   thermometer, turning every 5 minutes or so.
Depending on your grill, cooking should take 12 to 15
   minutes. Remove from grill and tent with foil and
   let chops rest for 8 minutes.
Serve with a 1/4 lemon slice. Serves 2.

Vegetable Shortcake

Submitted by Linda Livingston for Mary Thompson King

Shortcake:
2 cups flour
4 tsp. baking powder
1/2 tsp. salt
4 Tbsp. shortening
3/4 cup milk
1 cup grated cheese

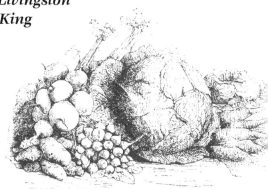

Mix well, adding cheese last.
Bake in 2 cake pans for 25 min at 375F.

Topping:
2 tbsp. shortening
1 large onion, chopped
1/2 cup celery, chopped
4 Tbsp. flour
4 Tbsp. water
1 large can tomatoes
1 cup cooked diced carrots
1 cup cooked green beans
Salt and pepper

Melt shortening; add onion and celery;
cook slowly until tender. Make a paste of flour
and water, add tomatoes and bring to a boil;
add paste; add carrots and green beans, salt and pepper.
Simmer 10 minutes. Serve over shortcake.
A family favorite.

MARY THOMPSON KING was an amazing woman full of love. She was always to be found in her kitchen making something awesome for her family. Family favorites include Vegetable shortcake, Seafood Chowder, cinnamon rolls, and the best two kinds of pie—warm and cold. She taught her family with her quiet grace to be strong, confident and to always love with your whole heart, unconditionally. To always see the best in others, no matter their faults. To always do whatever you could to help a friend, family member or a stranger in need. Everyone who met her is a better person because of her influence.

Vegetables & Sides

Charles Carpenter and Earnest Webster hoeing at C. W. Carpenter's
Strawberry Farm in 1905. Grant Ward Collection,
Museum & Arts Center in the Sequim-Dungeness Valley.

Braised Fennel and Bok Choi

Recipe by Karolina Tracz,
Submitted by Patty McManus

2 large fennel bulbs, rinsed clean
1 large bok choi
4 Tbsp.. butter
1 tsp. salt
1 tsp. sugar
2 Tbsp.. pastis or other anise-flavored liqueur
1/2 cup vegetable or chicken stock
1/2 cup water
2 Tbsp.. chopped fennel fronds
Zest from 1 orange
Lemon juice

Cut the tops off the fennel bulbs, chop 2 tablespoons of the fronds, and set aside. Slice the fennel bulbs in half lengthwise, through the core. Slice each half lengthwise into quarters, leaving some of the core attached so the pieces don't fall apart as they cook. Cut the bok choi in half.

Melt butter in a large pan over medium-high heat and place the fennel pieces in the pan in a single layer. Reduce heat to medium and cook without moving them for at least 2 minutes. Sprinkle the salt and sugar over the fennel. Check for browning, and cook for another minute or two if they're not browned yet. Turn the fennel pieces over and brown the other side.

Once the fennel bulbs are almost done, place the bok choi in the same pan and brown it the same as the fennel, but a lot quicker—one minute.

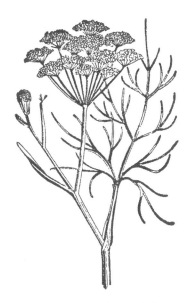

When both sides of the fennel are nicely browned, and the bok choi is cooked, add the liqueur to the pan.

Increase heat to medium high. The liqueur should boil down quickly. When it is almost gone, add the stock and water. Bring the liquid to a boil, then reduce the heat down to low, cover the pan and simmer for 15 minutes. Remove the cover, increase the heat to high and let the stock cook down until it is a glaze.

Add the fennel fronds and most of the orange zest and combine gently. Serve garnished with the rest of the zest and a few splashes of lemon juice or freshly sliced garlic.

Browned Broccoli

Recipe by Karolina Tracz
Submitted by Patty McManus

2 tablespoons oil
2 large stems of broccoli
1 large cauliflower
2 to 3 cloves garlic

Heat a skillet over medium heat. While it's heating, slice the garlic, broccoli and cauliflower from top to bottom into 1 inch slices. Toss in olive oil and sprinkle with salt and pepper. Place the veggies in a hot skillet, pressing them into the pan with a spatula. Cook them for 5 to 7 minutes, or until nicely browned. Once cooked, serve with shredded carrots or radishes.

KAROLINA TRACZ was born and raised in Poland and moved to Santa Barbara, CA, in her teens. On a road trip she fell in love with the Pacific Northwest and ended up moving to Seattle in 2005.

In 2009 she approached Nash's Organic Produce employees at a Seattle farmers market to see if she could become part of the farm team, and started helping at the U-District and Ballard markets.

In 2010, she moved to Sequim and started to work directly on the farm. In 2011, she also worked as the farm chef where she used her culinary skills to educate and nourish the community.

In her spare time, Karolina likes to go on bike rides, bake cookies, have picnics with friends, listen to music, go on adventures, and have fun!

Karolina says the rewarding aspects of working on the farm are getting to know the people who work there, enjoying the food grown in Dungeness, the kindness of simple everyday interactions, the sense of community, the last-minute dance parties, and learning about growing healthy, organic produce.

KAROLINA'S NICKNAME on the farm is "Grandma" because she loves taking care of everyone and feeding the people well. She made a farm lunch once per week all year long for the 2011 season.

The recipes presented here were developed by Karolina during the 2011 season, using Nash's fresh, organic vegetables.

Chioggia Slaw
on a bed of Grilled Leeks

Recipe by Karolina Tracz
Submitted by Patty McManus

Chioggia slaw

1/4 cup plain Greek-style yogurt
1 teaspoon finely grated orange zest
3 tablespoons fresh orange juice
1 tablespoon fresh lemon juice
5 candy-stripe (Chioggia) beets, julienned or grated
1 medium carrot, julienned or grated
Salt and freshly ground black pepper

Whisk yogurt, orange zest and juice, and lemon juice in a medium bowl. Add beets and carrot and toss to combine. Season to taste with salt and pepper.

Grilled Leeks

12 medium leeks, trimmed to about 7 inches,
split lengthwise to within 1-1/2 inches of the root end
Olive oil for grilling
Vinaigrette
4 teaspoons Dijon-style mustard
3 tablespoons white-wine vinegar
1/2 cup extra-virgin olive oil
1/3 cup minced assorted fresh basil

Tie the leeks in 4 bundles with kitchen string. In a kettle of boiling salted water, boil them for 6 minutes, or until they are just tender, and drain them in a colander. Refresh the leeks under cold water and discard the strings. Brush the leeks with the oil and grill them on an oiled rack set, 5 minutes on each side, or until they are golden.

Transfer the leeks to a platter as they are grilled and keep them warm. In a separate bowl combine all the vinaigrette ingredients and season with salt and pepper. Drizzle the vinaigrette over the leeks and top with Chioggia slaw.

Fava Bean Pesto on Charred Romaine Salad

Recipe by Karolina Tracz
Submitted by Patty McManus

1 cup fava beans (removed from pods and blanched)
1 bunch garlic scapes, roasted
4 tablespoons olive oil
lemon juice to taste (optional)
salt to taste
1 head Romaine lettuce

Preheat oven to 375F. Place garlic scapes on a cookie sheet with a little oil, roast for about 10 minutes. Remove from the oven and let them cool. Once cooled, place all ingredients, except Romaine, in a food processor and pulse till combined. Set aside.

Cut head of romaine lettuce in 4 wedges. Drizzle cut sides of the wedges with olive oil and sprinkle with salt and pepper. Grill the romaine over a hot fire, cut side down, until charred in spots, about 20 seconds. Turn the romaine over and grill for 20 seconds longer. Transfer the wedges to a platter, cut side up, and drizzle the fava bean pesto over them.

Grilled Golden Beets with Brown Butter Vinaigrette on a Bed of Fresh Greens

Recipe by Karolina Tracz
Submitted by Patty McManus

1 bunch golden beets,
   washed and cut into 1-inch slices
   (Keep the tops. Cut and reserve for salad)
1/2 cup olive oil
2 Tbsp.. smoked Hungarian or sweet paprika
1 tbsp. ground fennel
1 Tbsp. ground coriander
2 garlic cloves, minced
4 thyme sprigs or 2 Tbsp. ground thyme
4 Tbsp. unsalted butter
2 Tbsp. sherry vinegar or wine vinegar
1 Tbsp. water
1 bunch spinach
1 bunch reserved beet tops
1 bunch red leaf lettuce
1 bunch arugula
1 bunch romaine lettuce
1 bunch Italian parsley

In a bowl, combine olive oil, paprika, fennel, coriander, garlic and thyme. Add beets and marinate two hours.

Preheat a grill pan. Remove the beets from the marinade and sprinkle with salt and pepper. Grill on medium heat for 10 minutes until beets turn brown, then transfer to a bowl. Meanwhile cook butter until it turns brown and starts to have a nutty smell (about 5-10 minutes).

Add the sherry or wine vinegar and water. Mix well and season with salt and pepper. Add the vinaigrette to the beets and serve it on the bed of greens.

Greens

Chop the spinach, beet tops, red leaf lettuce, arugula, romaine, and parsley into bite-sized pieces and combine in a bowl. Put a serving of greens on each plate and top with grilled browned buttered beets.

Kids' Favorite Kale Chips

Recipe by Karolina Tracz
Submitted by Patty McManus

12 large Lacinato
    kale leaves, rinsed,
    dried, cut lengthwise
    in half, center ribs
    and stems removed
1 tablespoon olive oil
Salt and pepper to taste

Preheat oven to 350F.
Toss kale with oil in
large bowl. Sprinkle with
salt and pepper. Arrange
leaves in single layer on
two large baking sheets.
Bake until crisp, about
15 minutes for flat leaves,
up to 20 minutes for
wrinkled leaves. Transfer
leaves to bowl to cool. Enjoy!

Nash's Kale Slaw

Recipe by Karolina Tracz
Submitted by Patty McManus

1 bunch Nash's red kale, shredded
2 carrots, shredded
1 small red or Walla Walla onion, minced
2/3 cup olive oil
1/3 cup balsamic vinegar
1 tablespoon fresh lime juice
1 teaspoon maple syrup
1 pinch salt
1 pinch ground black pepper

Stir together kale, carrots, and onion in a very
large bowl; set aside. Whisk together olive oil, vinegar,
lime juice, maple syrup, salt, and pepper. Pour the
dressing over the vegetables, and stir thoroughly,
making sure to coat the vegetables very well.
Chill in the refrigerator for two hours before serving.

Oil and Vinegar Potato Salad

Recipe by Karolina Tracz
Submitted by Patty McManus

1 1/2 pounds russet potatoes
(about 5 medium), unpeeled and boiled
1/4 cup red wine vinegar
1/2 teaspoon sugar
1/2 small red onion, very thinly sliced
1/4 cup extra-virgin olive oil
2 tablespoons chopped fresh Italian parsley

Quick Summer Kale Apple Sauté

Recipe by Karolina Tracz
Submitted by Patty McManus

1 Granny Smith apple
2 tablespoons olive oil
1 medium onion, cut into 1/4-inch wedges
1/4 teaspoon curry powder
1 lb. kale, tough stems and ribs removed
    and leaves coarsely chopped
1/2 cup water

Peel, quarter, and core apple, then cut into 1/4-inch-thick wedges. Heat oil in a 5-quart pot over moderately high heat until hot but not smoking, then sauté onion, stirring occasionally, until golden. Add apple and curry powder and sauté, stirring, until apple is almost tender, about two minutes. Add kale and water and cook, covered, stirring occasionally, until kale is tender and most of the liquid has evaporated, about 10 minutes. Season with salt.

Roasted Beet Salsa with Skillet-Browned Broccoli

Recipe by Karolina Tracz
Submitted by Patty McManus

4 medium golden beets
4 tablespoons extra virgin olive oil
Salt and pepper
2 teaspoons shallots, finely diced
2 teaspoons fresh ginger, grated
1 teaspoon jalapeño, finely diced
1/2 teaspoon garlic, minced
1/4 cup fresh mint, minced
1/4 cup fresh cilantro, minced
2 teaspoons lime juice

To roast beets:

Preheat the oven to 375F. Trim tops off beets
and drizzle with olive oil. Season beets with salt
and pepper, wrap them in aluminum foil and
roast until tender, about 40-50 minutes.
Let cool in the foil.

While the beets are roasting, place the shallots,
jalapeño, ginger, garlic, mint, cilantro, lime juice
and 6 tablespoons of olive oil in a small bowl
and stir to combine.

When the beets are done, carefully remove the foil.
Peel them by slipping the skins off with your fingers.
Dice the beets and add salsa mixture, stirring to
combine. Taste for seasoning. Served on a bed
of arugula or spinach.

Basil/Onion Cream on Zucchini Pancakes

Recipe by Karolina Tracz
Submitted by Patty McManus

Cream

3/4 cup sour cream
2 tablespoons water
1/4 cup chopped fresh basil
2 tablespoons chopped green tops
  of Walla Walla onion
1/2 teaspoon salt, or to taste
Blend sour cream, water, basil,
  onion tops, and salt in a blender
  until smooth and pale green.
  Chill until ready to serve.

Pancakes

4 cups coarsely grated zucchini
1-1/4 teaspoons salt
1/4 cup Nash's soft white
  pastry flour
1-1/2 teaspoons sugar
1/4 teaspoon black pepper
2 large egg whites
4 tablespoons vegetable oil

Put zucchini in a colander and toss with salt.
Let stand at room temperature 20 minutes,
then wrap zucchini in a kitchen towel and get
out as much liquid as possible. Transfer zucchini
to a large bowl and stir in flour, sugar, and pepper.
Beat egg whites with a pinch of salt, then gently
fold into zucchini mixture.

Heat 2 tablespoons oil in a skillet over medium heat until hot but not smoking. Working in batches of five, spoon 2 tablespoons batter per pancake into skillet, flattening slightly with back of spoon. Cook pancakes, turning once, until golden brown, about three minutes total, transferring as cooked to paper towels to drain and adding more oil to skillet as necessary.

Top with basil/onion cream before serving.

The Three "P" Salad

Submitted by Mike Bare

As I remember it, we had this salad at most picnics and holiday meals. I always thought it was a family recipe, but my sister Pearl disagrees with me. She thinks Mom got it from a women's magazine in the 1950s. Either way, it is what I bring to most potlucks. It's very easy to make, and a little goes a long way.

1 (15 oz.) can of sweet peas, drained.
   I use the cheapest at the store.
7 oz. Spanish Peanuts. The skins are a bit bitter
   so rub small quantities of the peanuts between
   the palms of your hand to remove some of the skins.
6 oz. of pickles, diced to the size of the peas.
   I use Clausen's Kosher Dill, but use the pickles
   you like.
Several Tbsp. mayonnaise.

Place the peas, pickles, and Spanish peanuts in a medium sized mixing bowl, fold in enough mayonnaise to hold everything together. It's ready to eat; doesn't seem to need any seasoning.

Notes:

- Because the peanuts will soften in the mixture after a day or two, I prepare the ingredients beforehand, but don't mix them together until the day they'll be served.

- My sister Pearl uses Miracle Whip instead of mayonnaise. She prefers the tang.

- Spanish peanuts are very close to the pea in size, and their different taste works better for the salad. —*Mike Bare*

Mike and Kathy manage the Dungeness Schoolhouse, built in 1892 and owned by the Museum & Arts Center in the Sequim-Dungeness Valley. *Photo by Reneé Mizar.*

- "The combination is just so unusual. When I first heard pickles and peas were in it, I was like, Yuck! But when I tried it, it was so good." —*Kathy Bare*

MIKE AND KATHY BARE married in 2006 and retired to Sequim shortly thereafter. Together they are managers of the Museum & Arts Center's historical Dungeness Schoolhouse. Kathy is also involved with the Seattle Children's Hospital's Sequim Guild, American Sewing Guild, Stitches from the Heart, and Clallam County Genealogical Society. Mike volunteers at both the Sequim and Port Angeles Senior Centers, running ukulele groups, and plays ukulele with the *Washington Old Time Fiddlers.*

Mike Bare creates his Three "P" Salad. *Photo by Reneé Mizar.*

Several wagonloads of grain being threshed.
Photo from Frank and Bessie Lotzgesell Knopf, Verona Rice Collection,
Museum & Arts Center in the Sequim-Dungeness Valley.

Breads

Boston Brown Bread

Submitted by Ann Marie Kimler

1 cup bread flour
1 1/2 cup whole wheat flour
1/2 cup corn meal
1 cup molasses
1 1/2 cup buttermilk
1 tsp. baking soda
1 tsp. salt
2 tsp. sugar
2 tsp. margarine or butter
2/3 cups of soft raisins
1/4 cup or more chopped walnuts

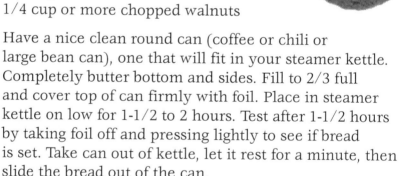

Have a nice clean round can (coffee or chili or large bean can), one that will fit in your steamer kettle. Completely butter bottom and sides. Fill to 2/3 full and cover top of can firmly with foil. Place in steamer kettle on low for 1-1/2 to 2 hours. Test after 1-1/2 hours by taking foil off and pressing lightly to see if bread is set. Take can out of kettle, let it rest for a minute, then slide the bread out of the can.

I WAS BORN IN Port Townsend in 1938 and moved to the Sequim area a few years later. My dad was a foreman for Hugh Govan Ranch and when I was young we lived at the ranch. We had beef cows, pigs, chickens, milk cows and other animals. My sister and I hauled hay to fill the big barn with winter feed for the animals. We had pits to put the hay in, to make silage.

My sister and I were always busy. If it wasn't weeding the garden or doing outside chores, we were helping Mom fix food for the hay hands in the summer. Cooking was all done on a wood stove where my mom always had homemade bread, rolls, and cottage cheese on the big stove—every day in the summer and winter.

We also did a lot of canning and it too was done on the wood stove, then put in the store house for our winter use. The garden and our livestock provided us with our year-round groceries. We even made our own soups. This bread recipe reminds me of my youth and working with my mom when she made the breads.

Dad in the garden.

Sourdough Bread with Nash's Triticale Flour

Submitted by Eliza Winne

Timeframe: 12-15 hours
Ingredients:
1-1/2 cups sourdough starter
5 cups Nash's Organic Triticale flour
4 cups water
1/3 cup organic olive oil
1 Tbsp. salt
4-6 cups organic unbleached white flour

Creating the Sponge

Combine sourdough starter, water and Nash's triticale flour in a large bowl, mix well and cover with a moist towel. Let this mixture sit at room temperature for 8 to 12 hours. This is the sponge. A sponge is basically feeding the sourdough starter with fresh flour and water while creating a medium that will make the bread rise. When the surface is bubbly, scoop out 1-1/2 cups of the sponge and place in a clean jar with a lid and refrigerate. This becomes your starter for the next batch of bread.

Making the Sourdough Bread

Now that some sourdough starter has been saved for future batches, stir into the sponge the olive oil and salt. Next, fold in the unbleached white flour, 1 cup at a time, until a dough forms. At this point the dough will begin to pull away from the edges of the bowl. Remove from the bowl and place on a floured counter-top. Knead for 10-15 minutes, adding flour when necessary to keep the dough from sticking to the counter. Kneading

Eliza Winne
and a fresh loaf
of her Triticale
Sourdough.

is complete when it becomes difficult to add more flour and the dough easily holds its form in a ball. Once dough is thoroughly kneaded, divide into 2 or 3 pieces, depending on how large you would like your loaves.

Place your loaves on an oiled cookie sheet or in bread pans, cover with a moist towel and let rise at room temperature for approximately 2 hours.

Preheat the oven to 400F. Sprinkle salt and makeslits on the surface of the loaves. Place loaves in the preheated oven for 20 minutes. After 20 minites turn the oven down to 375F and continue to bake 45-60 minutes. When the surface and bottom of the loaves are well browned, remove from the oven and tap with a knuckle on the bottom of the loaf. If it makes a hollow sound, the bread is done. Cool on racks and enjoy.

Alterations & Recommendations

For a heartier bread, replace the unbleached white flour with Nash's Organic soft white wheat flour. For more information on sourdough bread, starters and general bread-making techniques, I recommend:

The Tassaara Bread Book, by Edward Espe Brown
The Laurel's Kitchen Bread Book, by Laurel Robertson
Wild Fermentation, by Sandor Ellix Katz

GROWING UP, my mother made bread for our family every week; helping her is one of my first memories. I stood on a stool next to her so I could see over the counter. I'm sure I wasn't much help, but making bread is not only an act of combining ingredients. To create an exceptional loaf of bread requires a feel for the dough and how it will behave under certain circumstances. These are things I learned from my mother while standing on the stool in her kitchen.

As soon as I could I began making bread on my own and I haven't stopped. In college, where I studied human nutrition, an interest in fermentation was sparked in me. Naturally, I began experimenting with sourdough starters and sourdough bread.

It took a few years to create a resilient sourdough starter and a method of making sourdough bread that I was satisfied with. I have kept the same sourdough starter for 4 years now and it has never been healthier than it has since I began feeding it with Nash's Organic triticale flour. *Making bread with an organic, freshly ground, locally grown grain is as good as it gets!*

Gourmet Scout Rolls on a Stick

Submitted by Craig Ritchie

Buy refrigerator rolls. Buy Parkay squirt margarine. Take Scouts to a remote beach. A little before breakfast time, build a fire. Cut 'marshmallow roasting' sticks. Open rolls, wrap around stick. Roast like a marshmallow till browned. Carefully pull off the stick and squirt the margarine in the hole. Pass out the freshbaked rolls and listen to the *Yum's*.

FOR YEARS THIS IS what I used in the Olympics for Scout trips. Shi Shi Beach, Sand Point, Cape Alava, and other hikes became memorable gastronomic events. In the evening, the roasting sticks were used for hot dogs and, of course, marshmallows.

Sat Upon Bread

Submitted by Dave Platt

Mom loved picnics. This was one of her signature dishes. It blends grandkids, picnics, fun, and good food! For real fun, here's a great picnic idea to make ahead of time—it rides well! Serves 6 to 8.

Combine 1-2/3 cups chopped pimento stuffed olives, 1-1/2 cups chopped, pitted, black olives, 2/3 cup olive oil, 1 4 oz jar pimentos, drained and chopped, 1/3 cup minced fresh parsley, 2 Tablespoons drained capers, 1 tablespoon minced garlic, 1 tablespoon minced fresh oregano, (or 1 teaspoon dried), and salt and pepper to taste. This should be covered and put into the refrigerator overnight for flavors to blend.

Cut 12- or 18-inch round French or Italian Bread in half, forming top and bottom; remove centers leaving 1" thick shell. Brush inside of shells with some of the salad liquid. Press half the salad into the bottom shell, place 4 oz. thinly sliced Jack cheese, and 4 oz. grated mozzarella cheese over salad, press on remaining salad, cover with top shell of bread and press again. Wrap in several layers of foil. Have someone (a grandchild?) sit on it on the way to the picnic. Once there, cut sandwich into wedges and serve..

Sat Upon Bread.

Marian Platt's 80th Birthday.

FOR MORE THAN 25 YEARS, the name Marian Platt was synonymous with food and cooking in Sequim. In 1982, our Mom and Dad retired from work and moved to Sequim, to enjoy a new life. Mom loved to garden, picnic, and cook. She loved to write, too, which together became a new goal. In 1987, her first Food column appeared in the *Sequim Gazette.* Soon she was writing a weekly column, "Kitchen Korner," and never missed a deadline for 25 years. Mom realized her dream in 2002, by publishing her Sequim cookbook, *From My Kitchen Window.* In Mom's own words: "The only thing that rivals the scenery in the Pacific Northwest is the food. The Pacific Northwest has a style all its own. It's called Northwest Cuisine."

June was Mom's favorite month; she felt that it was the actual beginning of a new year. "In June the air is sweet with the fragrance of nearby strawberry fields, and from my kitchen window, I can see a sky so blue—like a bowl of blueberries. A sentimental time of the year—it evokes many childhood emotions—the gaiety of carefree days with no school, the laziness of summer days, reading, and munching on fresh fruit. Summer comes slowly to us in the Sequim Valley, but when it comes it has a delicious pleasure to it." Mom passed away in February 2012. Her last column ran in January 2012, ending a distinguished, and delicious, career.   —*Sue Cohn and Dave Platt*

Zucchini Bread with Taste Bud Popping Topping

Submitted by Bonnie and Phillip Kuchler

3 eggs
1 cup white sugar
1 cup brown sugar
3 tsp. vanilla
1 cup oil
2 cups grated zucchini
3 cups flour
1 tsp. baking soda
1/2 tsp. salt
3 tsp. cinnamon

Zucchini bread—sometimes part of the breakfast fare at Sea Cliff Gardens Bed and Breakfast.

Topping:

1/4 cup butter, melted
1/4 cup old-fashioned oats
1/4 cup white sugar
Cinnamon to taste

Mix wet ingredients, add zucchini. Mix dry ingredients, add to wet ingredients. Mix well. Pour into two greased loaf pans. Bake for about 40 minutes at 350F.

Mix topping and carefully spread on loaves. Then bake an additional 15-20 minutes, until toothpick comes out clean.

OUR SEQUIM STORY is like the tale of so many others who have migrated here—enchanted by the sea, charmed by fields of lavender, courted by the rain shadow of the Olympic Mountains. We found Sequim

Waterfront gardens wedding of their son and new daughter in-law at the Bed and Breakfast of Bonnie and Phillip Kuchler in July 2012.

in the lavender-gorged summer of 2007. I remember when I saw those shades of purple backdropped by the snow-frosted Olympics. *I want to live here,* I thought. *This could be home!* In 2009, after packing our lives into one 40-foot container and three tiny dog crates, we moved from Hawaii to Sequim. We often say we came from Paradise to Heaven.

It's not easy, midlife, to start over. We knew we'd need a house, we'd need jobs, we'd need friends. The answer to all three wishes came from a bed & breakfast. Turnkey, we purchased a waterfront B&B on an acreage flush with flowers, west of Sequim. Our container of stuff arrived on Tuesday, and we served breakfast to a full house on Friday. That was 4,000 guests and countless loaves of zucchini bread ago.

THIS SUMMER my son and his beautiful bride were married at the B&B. As they voiced their vows on the edge of the cliff, surrounded by blue sky, blue water and friends, a bald eagle floated by, offering its blessing. This precious moment—along with so many other new memories and new friends—added a page to our own Sequim history book. And with each new chapter, the thought comes again . . . *Yep, we are home.*

Mary Petroff Collection,
Museum & Arts Center in the Sequim-Dungeness Valley.

Desserts

Anne's Scotch Cookies

Submitted by R.G. "Rick" Godfrey

Still a family favorite to this day!

Mix:
1 cup and 2 tablespoons sugar
3 cups oatmeal
2 cups flour
1/4 teaspoon salt

Add:
1/2 cup butter
1/2 cup Crisco
1 teaspoon baking soda
  dissolved in
  1/2 cup hot water

Mix like pie crust. Roll thin.
Bake at 370F for 12 minutes.

ANNE W. AND WILLIAM B. RITCHIE were leading citizens of Port Angeles, Washington. Anne was born in Belfast, Ireland, while William was born in Ayshire, Scotland. They were married in Scotland and arrived n Port Angeles on June 16, 1888, where they raised five children. Anne was well known for her involvement in social and charity organizations. William served his community in such positions as Deputy Sheriff of Clallam County and Prosecuting Attorney. He later became a judge in the Superior Court and after that was elected Mayor of Port Angeles. He represented the Clallam Tribe on many legal matters including obtaining compensation for their land use by passing a bill through Congress. He was also credited with obtaining the 99 year lease on Ediz Spit for the City of Port Angeles from the U.S. Government.

Ann W. and
William B.
Ritchie.

William B. Ritchie.

Applesauce Cookies

Submitted by
R. G. "Rick" Godfrey

1/2 cup shortening
1 cup raisins
1 cup nuts
1 cup sugar
1 cup applesauce
1 egg
1 tsp. soda
1/2 to 3/4 tsp. salt
2 cup flour
1/2 tsp. cinnamon
1/4 tsp. cloves

George and
Margaret Ann.

Cream shortening and sugar, add egg, then applesauce and soda. Sift dry ingredients and add to mixture. Drop from spoon onto greased cookie sheet. Bake at 375F. Ice with powdered sugar frosting while still hot.

"This is the boys' favorite." —*Margaret Ritchie Godfrey*

The Godfrey House on Maple Street.

Margaret R. & Herbert E. Godfrey.

MARGARET RITCHIE was born in Port Angeles, Washington. Her husband, Herbert, emigrated from Steppingley, England in 1903. Margaret was very active in starting the Episcopal Church in Sequim and wrote the history of the church, which is on file in St. Lukes on Fifth Avenue. In 1910 Herbert started the Knight-Godfrey Hardware Store at 131 Washington Street. The original building is still there today. He was town treasurer for Sequim for approximately 20 years until the town was incorporated. Herbert also served as the mayor of Sequim. Margaret served for many years as a Red Cross Leader during the war, a charity sponsor, and raised two children (George and Margaret Ann) in their home on Maple Street, which is still there today. Herbert was an avid gardener and had one of the best rose gardens on the Olympic Peninsula.

Blackberry Cobbler

Submitted by Ann Perkins

Crust:
2 cups flour
8 Tbsp butter and 3 Tbsp
  vegetable shortening
1/2 tsp. salt
Pinch of sugar
5 – 6 Tbsp cold water

Place all crust ingredients except water in a large bowl,
and rub the flour and fat together with your fingers
until small pieces form (about the size of oatmeal flakes)
Add the water and blend quickly with one hand,
gathering the dough into a ball. It should hold together,
but not be damp and sticky. Knead briefly with heel
of one hand to form into fairly smooth, round ball.
Cover with wax paper and refrigerate for two hours
or overnight. It will keep refrigerated for 3 or 4 days.

Filling:
About 6 cups blackberries (preferably picked by hand)
Grated zest of one lemon
1 Tbsp fresh lemon juice
1/2 to 2/3 cup granulated sugar
  depending on how sweet you like it
1 tsp. vanilla
1/2 tsp. culinary lavender,
  mashed in a mortar and pestle (optional)
2 Tbsp cornstarch
2 Tbsp butter

Remove crust from refrigerator. Preheat oven to 375F.
Place berries, vanilla, lemon rind and juice, and
lavender (if using) in a large bowl. Whisk sugar and
cornstarch in small bowl to combine, add to berries,

and place the mixture in a 2-quart baking dish.
Cut the butter into small pieces and distribute over
top of berries. Roll out crust to fit top of baking dish,
and cover berry filling, tucking the sides inside the dish.
Cut a few slits in the crust, and sprinkle lightly with
sugar. Bake any extra crust separately. Bake the cobbler
until fruit juices bubble up around the edges, about
30 to 35 minutes. Serve warm with vanilla ice cream
and a piece of extra crust on the side.

I GREW UP IN Kennesaw, Georgia, a small town like
Sequim. My husband Dave and I have enjoyed our
summers in Sequim since 2005 very much—hiking
with friends, taking advantage of the bounty of produce
and seafood from the area, and visiting places like
the Dungeness River Center, the Dungeness Spit,
and the Olympic Game Farm with our grandchildren.

My one contribution to Sequim so far is the motto
for the Centennial, "Get into the Sequim of Things."
Yes, I know that sounds unlikely, but it came about
this way: My friend Gretha Davis mentioned that the
Centennial Committee was looking for a slogan, and
I casually tossed out the suggestion "get into the Sequim
of things." We laughed and I thought no more about it,
until she told me a few months later that the slogan had
been adopted. I suppose she mentioned it to someone
on the committee, and they liked it! So now I am
proudly sporting the slogan on my license plate holder,
on the black Centennial vest, and on numerous stickers.
My family always picked blackberries in the summer in
the field behind our house in Georgia, and I was
delighted when we came to Sequim to find fields of
blackberries everywhere. Blackberry cobbler was one
of my favorite desserts as a child, and the recipe is
similar to the one I used to enjoy, with some minor
adaptations.

Carrot Cheesecake

Submitted by the Staff at Nash's Organic Produce

Crust

3/4 cups finely crushed graham crackers
2 Tbsp. chopped nuts (optional)
1 Tbsp. Nash's soft white flour
1 Tbsp. sugar
2 Tbsp. butter, melted

Stir together in medium bowl and press into bottom
of spring-form pan or bottom and sides of pie pan.

Cream Cheese Mixture

2 eight-ounce packages of cream cheese
   or créme fraiche
3/4 cup sugar
3 Nash's eggs

Beat cream cheese and sugar together till fluffy,
add 3 eggs and beat till smooth. Put one cup
of this mixture in a bowl and set the rest aside.

Carrot Mixture

2 cups pureed Nash's Best carrots
   that have been roasted or steamed
1 Nash's egg
1/4 cup Dungeness Creamery milk or cream
1/2 tsp. cinnamon
1/4 tsp. ginger

Here's a really unusual way
to use Nash's sweet carrots!
In a cheesecake!

To the 1 cup of cream cheese mixture,
add carrots, 1 egg, milk, spices.
Mix together and pour into pie crust.
Pour the reserved cream cheese mixture
over the top and run a knife through it.
swirling to create marbling.

Bake at 350F for 45 minutes till center
appears set when gently shaken.

Chill 4 hours before serving ...

(That never happens! Ha! Ha!)

Easy Chocolate Torte

Submitted by Karen Kuznek-Reese

1 (2 layer) pkg. chocolate cake mix
2 (4 oz.) pkg. Baker's German sweet chocolate
3/4 cup butter, softened
1/2 cup chopped toasted almonds
1 (8 oz.) container Cool Whip topping, thawed

Prepare cake mix as directed and bake in
2 greased and floured 9-inch layer pans.

Melt 1-1/2 packages of chocolate in saucepan over
very low heat. Cool; then beat in butter. Add almonds.

Make chocolate curls from remaining chocolate.
After cakes cool, split horizontally.

Spread 1 cake layer with half the chocolate mixture,
top with cake layer, spread half the whipped topping.

Repeat layers; garnish with chocolate curls.
Chill one hour.

My daughter Alicia, my parents (Bill & Helen Kuznek),
Alicia's friends, Matt Chartier, Colby Gallinger,
Kelsey Meyer, and Mikaela Murphy
all at our house for Alicia's birthday.

EACH YEAR I WOULD ask my daughter what
kind of cake she wanted for her birthday. When
she was young, she would want an ice cream cake.
For those birthdays she would also spend most
of the time hiding under the dining room table
and crying. Thank goodness she outgrew that
birthday reaction. When she got older, birthdays
were a lot more fun. This is the cake she would
usually request.

German New York Jersey Cheesecake

Submitted by Tawana Borden

Preheat oven
   to 400F

Use a 9 inch
springform pan

Crust

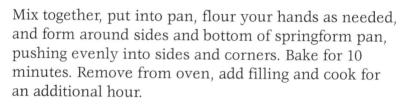

1 cup plus 2 Tbsp flour
5 Tbsp butter
3 Tbsp sugar
1 egg
1/2 tsp. baking powder
Lemon peel from a whole lemon
1/2 tsp. vanilla

Mix together, put into pan, flour your hands as needed, and form around sides and bottom of springform pan, pushing evenly into sides and corners. Bake for 10 minutes. Remove from oven, add filling and cook for an additional hour.

Filling

Two 8 oz. packages plus one 3 oz. package
   of softened Cream Cheese
1 cup half & half
1 cup minus 2 Tablespoons sugar
Juice of one lemon
4 eggs
3 Tablespoons cornstarch

Mix together just until combined (the more you mix the fluffier and lighter the filling becomes and isn't as good.)

BEING A MILITARY FAMILY and living all over, we enjoyed many different cultures. We were stationed in Wiesbaden, Germany in the 80's and we met some awesome folks, both fellow military and locals.

My husband is from New Jersey and misses some of his favorite foods from the East Coast; I was always on the hunt for a good recipe for a New York Cheesecake that would take him back to the good old days.

I worked with an awesome local named Leo, at the Schierstein Compound Café where Joe was stationed. I worked part time as a short order cook. We became friends and I was telling him that I was looking for a cheesecake recipe and he told me his girlfriend had an awesome one and for us to come over for dinner and she would make one for us.

WE COULDN'T REFUSE such a gracious invitation. He just forgot to mention that she spoke NO English (and he spoke broken English). Nevertheless we had a wonderful day with them at what they call their garden plot—really nice small areas they own with all the good things they can grow plus a small cabin-type building (with all the comforts). They had apple trees that the kids got to climb up and pick apples, which they loved.

The cheesecake and the whole meal was fantastic. I asked her for the recipe and she assured me she would write it down and send it with Leo. Boy did she. It was to my dismay written in GERMAN with METRIC MEASUREMENTS. Oh boy, did I have my work cut out for me, and Leo was not much help with the measurements as he only knew metric.

Grandma Dean's Soft Gingerbread Cookies

Submitted by Cindi Dean Watstet

This recipe is from Arabella Williams Dean; it makes a large batch of great soft gingerbread cookies.

1 cup shortening
1 cup sugar
1 egg
1 cup molasses
4 teaspoons baking soda
2 teaspoons ginger
2 teaspoons cinnamon
1/2 teaspoon cloves
1/4 teaspoon nutmeg
1 teaspoon salt
6 cups flour
1 cup buttermilk or sour milk

Cream together shortening and sugar. Sift together dry ingredientsand add egg and molasses, buttermilk or sour milk. Chill. Roll out and cut into shapes. Bake eight to ten minutes on *greased* cookie sheet at 375F.

THIS RECIPE WAS SHARED with me from my cousin Eileen Croxford, the great-granddaughter of Nellie Arabella, who was the wife of Jesse Martin Dean, the son of Benjamin Franklin Dean and Nancy Mariah Armstrong. The Deans were a Clallam County pioneer family, arriving in 1877. In addition to Jesse, they had six other children: James Curtis, Frederick Charles, Orville Vernon, Alma Myrtle, Daisy Maude and Charlotte Evelyn. The Dean family settled first at Cannery Point, near Sequim Bay, south of Washington Harbor, and had a homestead on Palo Alto Road. Between 1879 and 1902, they operated the cannery, a store, post office and the area's first telephone line. According to local and family legend, the town of Blyn was named after son, Orville. A neighbor could not pronounce Orville's first name, and called him Oblyn. As a tribute to his son, Ben shortened the nickname to Blyn. Dean Creek, just west of Blyn is named for the Dean family. The Deans sold all of their holdings in 1902 and moved to Seattle, where most of the family is buried. There are dozens of Dean great-grandchildren still living in western Washington, including in Sequim and Port Angeles.

The Dean Family.

Gramma Reandeau's Cinnamon Rolls

Submitted by Judy Reandeau Stipe

1 cup whole milk
1 package dry yeast
2 eggs
1/3 cup margarine
1 tsp. salt
1/2 cup sugar
4 cups all-purpose flour

Dissolve yeast in warm milk in large bowl. Stir in sugar, salt, eggs and melted margarine, then add flour and mix well. Knead the dough into a large ball (you'll need extra flour for your hands). Cover bowl and let sit for about an hour in a warm place until dough has doubled in size. On a lightly floured surface, roll dough out into a large rectangle (about 1/4 inch thick). Spread 1/3 cup soft margarine on the dough, sprinkle 1 cup packed brown sugar and 2 tbs. (or more) of cinnamon. Carefully roll up dough as tightly as possible & cut into 2-inch wide slices. Place on non-stick or buttered baking pan, cover and let rise for 30 minutes.

Bake 18 to 20 minutes in a 375F oven. Turn upside-down onto serving plate so syrup runs over the rolls and serve immediately. These are so sweet they don't really need frosting, but Gramma sometimes made a white gooey topping out of 8 tbs. of soft butter, 1-1/2 cups powdered sugar, dash of salt, 1/2 tsp. vanilla. and 1/4 cup cream cheese. Gramma always used butter in her baking because she churned her own, but I substitute margarine because the rolls turn out lighter.

MY FIRST MEMORY of my grandmother was connected to the smell of her cinnamon rolls when I was visiting the big house on the farm across the tracks from the railroad depot in Carlsborg. She made millions of cinnamon rolls for family, friends, workers, or passengers who stopped at the train depot.

May Cecilia Sell Reandeau.

May Cecilia Sell Reandeau was born in Kansas in 1899 and came to the area in the early 1930s with her husband, Thomas Lison Reandeau, their five children, and all the belongings they could carry in an old Dodge, to escape the "dust bowl" of South Dakota. They heard that fruit, berries, and vegetables would grow where you dropped seeds. Gramma said she was happy to move somewhere that her flowers and gardens would easily grow.

Friends settled on Whidbey Island wrote weekly letters about feeding themselves from the clams, oysters, crab and fish that were outside their door. Gramma smoked salmon, canned clams, fried oysters, harvested quarts of honey, raised thousands of chickens and sold eggs with a huge smile because she loved her new home in Carlsborg.

Thanks, Gramma, from your granddaughter,
—*Judy Reandeau Stipe*

Inge's Fresh Fruit Cake

Submitted by Laura Dubois

1- 1/3 cups flour
2/3 cup sugar
2 teaspoons baking powder
2/3 cup milk
1/4 cup butter, room temperature
2 eggs
1 teaspoon vanilla
Fresh Fruit
   (sliced peaches, nectarines, apples, plums, or berries)

Preheat oven to 350F. Combine dry ingredients; add milk, butter, egg and vanilla. Beat on low until combined. Beat on medium for one minute.

Pour batter into a greased and floured 8 x 8 pan. Place lots of sliced fruit or berries on top of the batter. (You can sprinkle some cinnamon on top of apples or peaches.)

Bake for 35 to 40 minutes or until a toothpick inserted in the center comes out clean. Serve with whipped cream or ice cream.

THIS IS MY ADAPTATION of my friend Inge Magrs' "150 Gram Cake," which is done in metric measures. Inge has a large garden and orchard in the Sequim-Dungeness Valley. She has shared many of her berries and orchard fruits with me and my husband in recent years. I adapted her recipe to use "cup and teaspoon" measurements and added more leavening for a lighter cake.

You can use any fresh fruit in season—or frozen fruit. It's a quick and easy way to enjoy local fresh fruit and berries any time. Inge's favorites are apples or peaches. My favorite is a combination of nectarines and berries. I have even tried strawberries and rhubarb.

Inge's Fresh Fruit Cake with Nectarines and blueberries.

Violet Grall's
Sour Cream Cutouts

Submitted by Violet Grall,
from a recipe of Lottie Winters, her mother

1 cup butter
  at room temperature
1-1/2 cups sugar
3 eggs
1 cup sour cream
2 teaspoons vanilla
3-1/2 cups flour
1 teaspoon baking powder
1 teaspoon baking soda
1/2 teaspoon salt

Blue Mountain School.

Cream together butter and sugar. Beat in eggs.
Add sour cream and vanilla; mix well. Mix dry
ingredients in separate bowl, then add to cream mixture.
Chill two hours or overnight. Roll on heavily floured
board to 1/4" thickness. Cut with 3" cutter and place
on lightly greased cookie sheet. Bake in 350F oven
for two minutes. Cool and lightly frost.

LOTTIE GREW UP on Blue Mountain and went to
Blue Mountain School. Her husband John Winters was
born in 1886. He was from a pioneer family who settled
in the Deer Park Road area in 1884. He and Lottie
met at a dance at Blue Mountain School and married
in 1910. They lived on and farmed the Winters
homestead. They had a herd of dairy cows and
raised five children.

Irv Boyd's Double Crust Pear Pie

Submitted by Magdalena Bassett

1 deep pie dish
2 round pie crusts to fit the dish
Irv used store-bought crust, but I'd encourage people
to use their own crust recipes.

Peel and slice 4 cups pears

Mix
3/4 cup brown sugar
3 tablespoons flour
1/4 teaspoon ground nutmeg
1/2 teaspoon rum extract
1/3 cup cream

Thinly slice 2 tablespoons of butter
  (put it in the freezer for 10 min. before slicing)
Place one crust in the bottom of the pie dish. Arrange
the pears evenly over the crust. Pour mixed ingredients
over the pears. Dot with butter slices. Cover with the
second crust and seal edges. Cut vent slits on top.
Place in preheated oven at 450F for 10 minutes,
lower the heat to 350F, and bake additional 40 minutes.
Serve warm.

IRVIN BOYD, born January 31, 1914 in Mt. Pleasant,
Washington, graduated from Joyce school in 1934,
ran pack trains in the Olympics, was a livestock dealer
and cattle rancher, and moved to Sequim in 1957.
He was an honorary Grand Pioneer in 2008. After
retiring, Irvin traveled extensively with his wife
Hellen, making Sequim their permanent base.
Irv died on Sept. 11, 2010, at the age of 96.

Margaret's Yum-Yum Cake

Submitted by David Lotzgezell

1 Cup Quick Cooking Oatmeal
1-1/4 Cups Hot Water
1/2 Cup Shortening
1 Cup White Sugar
1 Cup Brown Sugar
2 Eggs
1 teaspoon Vanilla
1/2 teaspoon Salt
1 teaspoon Baking Soda
1-1/2 Cups Flour
1 teaspoon ground Cinnamon

Icing Ingredients:
6 Tablespoons Butter
3/4 Cup Brown Sugar
4 Tablespoons Cream
1/2 Cup Coconut and Chopped Nuts (your choice)

Pour hot water on quick cooking oatmeal;
let sit while you mix other ingredients in another bowl.

In the main mixing bowl, cream together shortening,
sugars and eggs. Add vanilla, salt, baking soda, flour
and cinnamon. Add the soaking oatmeal and mix.
Pour into 8" x 8" greased pan and bake for 25-30 minutes
in preheated 350F oven.

Mix the icing ingredients together, spread over the
warm cake, place under the oven broiler until bubbly,
be careful not to burn the coconut & nuts. Watch closely.

Ready to serve! Best with vanilla ice cream.

The Lotzgezell Family.

Panukakua

Submitted by Suzie Bliven (Jarvis)

1 quart new milk
1 large cup of flour
1 tsp. salt
2 eggs

Beat all together until well blended and pour into a hot
buttered dish. Bake for 30 minutes in a 425 degree oven.
Enjoy with butter and real maple syrup.

THIS RECIPE WAS a favorite tradition in our Finnish
household as I was growing up. As you know, there
were many dairy farms here back in the day and
I was lucky enough to grow up on one in Agnew
(which was originally known as "Finn town" when
my grandparents lived here ... but that's another story.)

Panukakua was made using "new milk"—the colostrum milk from cows that had just "freshened" or just given birth to a new calf. The milk was really thick, dark yellow to almost orange, and often even had a bit of blood in it. It could not be put in with the milk that was going to market, so the cow was milked into a different bucket for us to enjoy, and for its baby calf to have a good start.

While I'm guessing the only way you could acquire some "new milk" today would to beg one of the two dairy farmers in our area for a quart, for this recipe you can probably substitute whole milk or even cream or half and half.

Gramma Olga and Grandfather Ero Jarvis carrying milk buckets on Finn Hill Farm.

Pennsylvania Dutch Shoe-Fly Pie (Molasses Crumb Cake)

Submitted by Ken Hays

Piecrust:

2 cups all-purpose flour
1 teaspoon salt
3/4 cup shortening
5 tablespoons water

Filling:

1/2 cup light molasses
1/4 cup brown sugar
1 egg, beaten
1/2 teaspoon baking soda
1/2 cup hot water

Crumb Topping:

1 cup all-purpose flour
3 tablespoons shortening
2/3 cup light brown sugar, packed
1 pinch salt
1 pinch ground cinnamon
1 pinch ground nutmeg

Directions:

For crust: In a medium bowl mix flour and salt. Cut shortening into flour mixture until it resembles coarse crumbs. Gradually add water until combined. Press together to form dough and chill at least 1 hour or overnight. Roll out dough on lightly floured surface to 1/8 inch thickness; fit into a 9 inch pie pan.

Preheat oven to 450 degrees F.

For filling: Combine molasses, brown sugar and egg. Dissolve baking soda in hot water, stir into syrup mixture and pour into crust.

For crumb topping: Mix dry ingredients together; cut in shortening until it forms crumbs. Sprinkle mixture over pie filling-*do not stir into filling mixture.*

Bake at 450 degrees F. for 15 minutes, then reduce heat to 350 degrees F. and bake 20 minutes longer or until toothpick comes out clean.

"It turns out Ann's Shoo-Fly Pie had many fans; competition was fierce."

text continues on page 165 ...

The hay-grass eaters . . .

WHEN I FIRST MOVED TO SEQUIM in 1977
I met my future wife Joanna Kimler and her family.
We shared a common bond of food and enjoyed many
meals together. Around the holiday season Joanna's
mom, Ann, would make Pennsylvania Dutch Shoo-Fly
pie. At the time molasses pie didn't really strike a
chord with me, so I dodged eating it. After Joanna
and I were married, these pies started coming to us
every holiday season. Evidently whenever Ann would
ask how I liked the pies Joanna told her that I really
loved them! Wanting to be the best son-in-law I could,
I eventually gave in and tasted one. Now I can't get
enough Shoo-Fly Pie.

About the time I discovered my obsession, Joanna
and I were having Thanksgiving dinner at her parents'
house every year. The extended family would gather:
Grandpa and Grandma Germeau, the kids and their
kids, and family friends. It turns out Ann's Shoo-Fly Pie
had many fans; competition was fierce. I had to find a
way to impress Ann, so I got to know Hubert Germeau,
my Grandpa-in-law. Hubert had a busy little farmstead
and I figured if I helped him out Ann would be *really
impressed* so I spent many summer afternoons putting
up hay bales with soft city hands.

Joanna and I live on the family farmstead now.
We don't loft hay into the barn anymore, but I have
fond memories of helping Grandpa Germeau, being
a good son-in-law. When the holidays roll around
and mother-in-law Ann delivers my allocation of
two Shoo-Fly pies, I fondly think about Grandpa
Germeau, blisters, and those serene days.

May Venard's First Cake

Submitted by R.G. "Rick" Godfrey

Never fails! May be baked in layers, loaf or gem pans.
1 cup butter or Crisco
2 cups sugar
1 cup sweet milk
3 cups flour
1/2 cup cornstarch
2 teaspoons baking powder
4 eggs – yolks and whites beaten separately

Sift dry ingredients together 2 or 3 times.
Cream butter or shortening and sugar.
Add beaten egg yolks.
Add flour alternately with milk.
Fold in beaten whites and flavoring.
Use lemon, caramel, banana cream, chocolate,
coconut pie filling and whipped cream.
Can use any frosting according to flavor of cake.
Butter and flour pan.
Bake at 350F for 25 minutes.

OTTO J. AND MAY V. HENDRICKS made the trip
from Kansas to Washington state in 1921. Otto first
taught school in Napevine and Chehalis, and then
became superintendent of schools in Sequim. May
taught at and was the principal of the Dungeness School
House in the 1930s, where they lived in the third floor
apartment, raising two daughters, Margaret and Mildred.
They later moved to their home on the corner of
Sequim/Dungeness and Three Crabs Roads. They
raised vegetables and fruit and preserved everything

May and Otto Hendricks.

they grew. Nothing was wasted. They also owned a small rental guest cottage on the same property and it is still there today. One of May's hobbies was genealogy. In addition to being an educator, Otto was a fisherman and a hunter. Fish came from the Dungeness River and ducks from the surrounding area. After retirement the Hendrickses did a teaching tour in Neah Bay in the Indian schools where they also had time for their hobbies of beachcombing, rock collecting and Native American history.

Mom's Blackberry Dumplings

Submitted by Jerilyn Gilchrist-Smith

2 cups flour
2 tsp. baking powder
3/4 cup sugar
1 cup milk
Mix above ingredients together.

3 cups blackberries
1/4 pound butter
1 cup sugar (or more per taste)

Place berries into pan. Add sugar and butter. Bring to a boil.
Drop dumplings into mixture, cover, steam/simmer for approximately 20 minutes. Do not remove lid.
Serve hot with vanilla ice cream or whipped cream.

Mom served her blackberry dumplings with cream fresh from the dairy. Yum!

SEQUIM VALLEY was home to many dairy farms when I grew up in the 50s and 60s. Some of the good memories are riding bicycles with friends, running down the road to visit the neighbors, and fishing for trout in Johnson Creek with my older brother, Ken. Another good memory is going wild blackberry picking with my mom and younger siblings, Leah and Roger. We would carry our little buckets (previously containing lard, I think) and tramp through brush, over logs, fighting weeds and often falling into holes to find the precious little treasures. The sooner we filled our buckets, the faster we'd be able to go home, so we rarely ate them while we picked. We also knew we'd be enjoying them at home via Mom's dumplings later. I especially enjoyed Mom's Blackberry Dumplings with fresh cream from our dairy. Our brother Ken still has the berry buckets and we remember those times fondly.

Poor Man's Chocolate Cake

Submitted by Saundra Cutsinger

3 cups flour
2 cups sugar
2/3 cup cocoa
2 tsp. baking soda
1 tsp. salt
2 tsp. vinegar
2 tsp. vanilla
2/3 cup oil
2 cups cold water

Put all dry ingredients into an ungreased oblong pan and stir them all together. Next, with a spoon, make three large indentions (holes) in the dry ingredients. Put the vinegar in one hole, vanilla in another hole, and oil in the third hole. Then, pour the water into each hole and stir all together until smooth.

Bake at 350F for 35 minutes. Test with a toothpick that comes out clean.

After I took it from the oven, I mixed up some powdered sugar with some cocoa powder and a little vanilla and hot coffee. I stirred it up until it was a smooth consistency, close to smooth peanut butter, and immediately spread it on the cake. The warmth from the cake made it spread to a nice smooth surface that crusted around the edges when it cooled.

MY HUSBAND BELONGED to a gun club. One morning he told me he had volunteered me to make a cake for the picnic we were going to that day. So I whipped up this "Poor Man's Chocolate Cake" family

Saundra Cutsinger and her artwork.
Photo courtesy of *The Sequim Gazette.*

favorite that's easy to make when you don't have eggs or much time.

WHEN WE ARRIVED I asked which table the desserts for the picnic were to be on. They said over there, pointing at tables of fancy cakes. So I figured it must be a decorated cake contest and set mine down at the end, thinking nothing more about it.

Later, I heard my name being announced. I thought, "Who wants me?" I went to find out and they handed me a blue ribbon and said I had won the Best Tasting Cake contest. Was I shocked! There were at least four tables covered with all these fancy decorated cakes, beautiful to behold, and my plain cake, still in the pan I'd baked it in, was picked as the best tasting cake.

"Sweetsey's" Chocolate Mayonnaise Cake

Submitted by Judy Reandeau Stipe

Pour 1 cup boiling water over
1 cup chopped dates
1 cup chopped walnuts
1 tsp. baking soda
1 tsp. vanilla
Mix & let stand until cool.

In large bowl, blend 1 cup sugar, 1-1/2 cups flour,
2 tbsp. dark cocoa, 1 cup grated dark chocolate,
1/2 tsp. salt

Mix dry & wet ingredients by hand and fold in
1 cup of mayonnaise

Bake at 325F for about 50 minutes in rectangular glass
pan. Cover immediately to keep moist.

MY MOM DISCOVERED this chocolate mayonnaise
cake recipe during the 1950s when it was published
in the local paper. Although she didn't cook anything
complicated, she made this cake for all our friends.

Sonja Pearson (Bolewicki), our close neighbor, still
remembers this delicious but somewhat odd moist cake.
The delicacy became our birthday cakes for many years.
It can be frosted warm, which adds another layer of rich
goo, so a small piece goes a long way.

Mom didn't eat seafood, fish or much meat so we were
raised on eggs, chicken, turkey and tons of vegetables.
Her split pea soup and cauliflower casserole are my
favorites that I learned from her and still use for my
family. She later added meatloaf, spaghetti and roast

Lionne, Age 3, 1926.

beef to our menu to break up the week when we got older. When Dad was out of town on a logging job, we begged her for toasted cheese sandwiches for dinner and all four of us kids ate like wolves because she knew how to crisp up the outside perfectly while the Velveeta oozed out like hot lava. My mom's name was Lionne Gladys Burke and her grandparents landed at the Dungeness dock in 1898 by steamship. She married my dad, Ray Reandeau, and had Tommy, Judy, Bobby, and Patti Rae. Later she married George (Tuffy) Sands from Sekui, who took wonderful care of her in her remaining years.

Spritz Butter Cookies

Submitted by Barbara Collier Hanna

A cookie press is needed for this recipe.
One can be found at any good kitchen store.

Preheat oven to 400F.

1 cup butter or margarine, softened
1/2 cup sugar
1 egg
1 tsp. vanilla or almond extract
　　(I use vanilla)
1/2 tsp. salt
2 1/2 cups all-purpose flour
　　(not self-rising)

Cream butter and sugar together,
add egg and vanilla. Mix until
well blended. Combine salt and
flour and slowly add to wet mixture.

Fill cookie press with dough
and form into desired shapes.
Decorate the cookies with colored sugar.

Bake 6 to 9 minutes or until set, but not brown.
Makes approximately 5 dozen cookies.

For variation, you can add a couple drops of food
coloring to the dough , or for chocolate spritz cookies
add 1 oz. melted and cooled unsweetened chocolate
to the wet ingredients.

text continues on page 176 ...

Mom and Dad as newlyweds—Alice and Frank Collier.

WHEN I WAS a young girl growing up in Tacoma, my father worked shift work at the St. Regis Paper Mill. He was often working in the evenings, leaving Mom on her own to entertain her three young daughters. I am the youngest of the three, and I was about five years old when she began teaching us all how to embroider. She would take the money she made babysitting some of the neighborhood kids after school and walk us up to the "variety" store to buy iron-on patterns and yards of muslin. A year or so later, she taught us all how to read a pattern and crochet. We started using a big hook and yarn, but eventually graduated to fine thread and making doilies. I still enjoy both of these crafts.

While we did spend time watching television, I also remember spending a lot of time piled around Mom and reading from *The Children's Book of Knowledge*, a kind of condensed encyclopedia. I was always trying to keep up with my big sisters and wanted to do everything they did. I started reading at an early age, and it is still one of my favorite pastimes.

One of my fondest childhood memories was gathering around the kitchen table to make spritz cookies at Christmastime. The cookie press was made of metal and copper and we would take turns choosing the design and turning the press. Several years ago, my mom had surgery on her foot and we rotated caring for her that summer. For my birthday in September, she was upset that she hadn't been able to get out much

The Collier Sisters; Barbara, Debbie, and Julie.

to do any shopping. But she'd seen an ad for a cookie press and ordered it through the mail for me. I was thrilled and assured her it was a perfect gift.

Each holiday season I look forward to a full day of making cookies and especially the delicate, buttery and slightly sweet spritz cookies—our holiday tradition.

Index

Made in the USA
Middletown, DE
02 July 2016